Advance Review Copy: Conservation Confidential

A note to reviewers: Please remember that these proofs are uncorrected and that substantial changes may be made before the book is printed. If any material from the book is to be quoted in a review, please check it against the final bound book, which will be sent to you when it is ready. For media inquiries, speaking engagements, and book club queries, please contact Jon Gosch at Latah Books, jon@latahbooks.com

Conservation Confidential

Also by Mitch Friedman

Cascadia Wild: Protecting an International Ecosystem

Conservation Confidential:
A Wild Path to a Less Polarizing and More Effective Activism

Mitch Friedman

Conservation Confidential:
A Wild Path to a Less Polarizing and More Effective Activism

Copyright 2025 by Mitch Friedman

All rights reserved. No portion of this book may be reproduced in any form without permission from the publisher, except as permitted by U.S. copyright law.
For permissions, contact: editor@latahbooks.com

Book design by Russ Davis, www.BravoBookDesign.com
Cover design by Tyler Ung

Cover image used with permission from Archives & Special Collections, Western Libraries, Western Washington University —Fishtown0102a

Trade paperback ISBN: 978-1-957607-40-5
Hardcover: 978-1-957607-39-9
eBook: 978-1-957607-41-2

Cataloging-in-Publication Data is available upon request

Manufactured in the United States of America

Published by Latah Books
www.latahbooks.com

Contents

Part I: Ancient Forest Wars
1. Empowerment 2
2. Roots and Sprouting 8
3. From Radical Action to Radical Impact 22
4. Learning from Success and Failure 32
5. Saving the Forest Through the Trees 42

Part II: Collaboration
6. Collaboration: Its Origin Story 58
7. Finding Common Ground in the Woods 68
8. Wolves Bring Out the Best and Worst in People 80
9. Coexisting with Wolves 98
10. Better Beef 104
11. Hunting for Solutions 112

Part III: Conservation Principles
12. Forests and People 122
13. What Muir and Leopold Got Wrong 130
14. Land and Wildlife Management by Native Peoples . 142
15. Helping Government Succeed 154
16. What Brower and Foreman Got Wrong 164

Part IV: Coexistence
17. Hope, Heritage, and Habitat Connections 172
18. From Polarization to Progress in Okanogan County 184
19. Conservation, Citizenship, and Democracy 190
20. Advocacy: Doing Something Is Better Than Being Something 202
    Epilogue: Going Forward 209

Regional Map of Work Area

Note on terminology: I use multiple terms for Native people. While it's common in the U.S. to reference Native American Tribes, in Canada the accepted phrase is First Nations. I use both accordingly. I also generalize with the term Natives or Native peoples. But mostly I use the term Indian, following what I notice is the preference of my Indian friends on both sides of the border.

Part I

Ancient Forest Wars

1

Empowerment

Lon getting a rope onto my tree at Millennium Grove
(photo by the author)

"I can't do it. It's too hard," cried out Mokai from the distance, obscured from view by gigantic Douglas fir trees standing between us.

It was June of 1985 in the Millenium Grove, among the oldest old-growth forests in all of Oregon, with trees approaching a millennium in age, as wide as a basketball hoop is tall, and a football field in height. Such forests once blanketed much of the Pacific Northwest, but a century of relentless logging had decimated their extent, replacing trees and forests that stood tall even before America's founding with clearcuts and plantations of relatively young trees. The grove stood on national forest land in the Cascade Mountains an hour drive east of Corvallis. It is where tree-sitting was first tried as a tactic to block logging of old-growth or "ancient forest." That first climb was done by two people just two weeks earlier. Now, six of us were to climb up into the canopies of six different trees before loggers returned in the morning. Six trees, six climbers, six different techniques, so we could learn what worked best.

Poor Mokai had it the worst. He was using a sledgehammer to pound giant nails deep enough into his tree that they could support his weight. From each nail he hung a strand of webbing with foot loops that served as a ladder. He set his feet into the one hanging from his most recent nail while pounding the next nail a foot or two higher, onto which he would then hang a second webbing ladder and thus ascend. The catch is that old-growth trees have dense outer wood that resists nails. Mokai, a skinny California hippie in his thirties, was struggling.

I had an easier climbing assignment. The tactic for my tree was to shoot an arrow—with string attached—up and over the lowest branch, some eight stories up. Use the string to pull a rope over the branch, and you're all set to climb that rope using two jumars, a hand-held tool that slides along the rope and, again, has webbing attached for foot placement.

The two activists who adapted these techniques were, like me, in their early twenties. They happened to be avid rock climbers. Mikal, from Wenatchee, Washington, who had a manic giggle to match the frenetic storm in his mind, was going by the arboreal pseudonym Doug Fir. Val Wade, his calmer, athletic girlfriend from western Oregon, went by the more-floral Rhoda Dendron.

I had taken the name Bruce Budworm (a play on spruce budworm, a forest insect). Lon, another journeyman California hippie with no pseudonym, was supporting me. These guys had experience in the methods of nonviolent civil disobedience. I was a neophyte.

Lon had a barrel-chest and long black hair. He also had a big joint in the corner of his mouth as he leaned back, aimed his bow skyward in a pose fitting for *Zen in the Art of Archery*, and loosed an arrow. It skyed to loop over the branch even as we heard the futile clanging of Mokai's hammer.

As daylight waned, I asked Lon, "What if this doesn't work and we don't get up in the trees?"

"That doesn't matter," replied this sage from the 1960s. "What matters is that you're getting empowered."

Boom!

Each of us has tremendous agency. Our form of government gives us the right and opportunity to exercise unlimited influence. I despair that we don't do enough in America to prepare people on how best to use their agency for the greater good. Empowerment is the first step in that process.

We all successfully climbed those trees, even Mokai. I spent two or three nights on a two-foot-by-six-foot sheet of plywood hanging slipshod from that big branch, suffering a mild headache from being unable to keep my head higher than my feet. Memories fade over 40 years' time, but a chill pervaded that canopy, which little sunshine penetrated. It was thankfully windless and still, with tints of green and brown monopolizing my view. Tree-sitting is not suited to a claustrophobe or vertigo sufferer. Thankfully, I am neither.

A picture of me high in that tree, a banner hanging from my platform, ran on the front page of regional newspapers. This creative escalation of the nascent ancient forest war was big news.

After my modest stint of treacherous yet tedious dangling, I abandoned my tree for a summer fisheries job in the Bering Sea. I descended, but the protest continued for a couple weeks before police and loggers prevailed. The oldest trees in Oregon fell, leaving giant stumps in a landscape replete with them. Nonetheless, Lon was right. I had been empowered. I entered fully into the epic and historic battle to preserve the Northwest's last-standing ancient forests, and from there to championing its larger ecosystems and iconic wildlife. I spent the ensuing decades in conservation work, the first three years of it on the radical edge.

Today, I lead a nonprofit organization I founded thirty-five years ago to protect the wildlands and wildlife of Washington State and adjacent parts of British Columbia, Canada. I work directly with three dozen amazing people, several with decades of tenure.

We have played substantial roles in the successful protection of most of the Northwest's remaining ancient forests and wild areas and established functioning habitat corridors—including the means for wildlife to safely cross highways—that are adding up to a connected ecosystem across our regional landscape. We have helped return several iconic carnivores—gray wolf, Pacific fisher, wolverine, Canada lynx, and hopefully soon, grizzly bear—to areas from which they had been absent for generations. This conservation progress came even as Washington, the smallest western state with the least amount of public land, saw its human population and economy boom.

I am fortunate to have had the opportunity to engage and succeed in the mission of nature conservation that has always been my calling. That climb into the canopy of the Millenium Grove was my empowering entrée into one of the world's greatest conservation battles—saving the Northwest's ancient forests. I took on the role of firebrand, an energetic leader on the edges of radical thought and action. From there, I learned and evolved. The things we have accomplished, the wild nature that we have protected, are great in scale and gratifying in spirit. I have the satisfaction of knowing that, in a world aflame, I have done more than my share to find and follow a path to a better, more sustainable future.

But I am also frustrated. Many of my peers in conservation and activism in general allow passion and virtue signaling to override their interests, making choices and statements that look better in headlines and fundraising appeals than on the ground. Needless polarization alienates allies and pollutes democracy, serving nature poorly in the process.

I relate to the sense of urgency. Desperate times do call for desperate measures, but preferably effective ones. When I came of age, our ancient forests and roadless areas were under full assault by government and industry, habitat corridors and wildlife highway crossings were mere theory, and few gave any thought to large carnivores in the Pacific Northwest, as wolves and wolverines were long gone and forgotten. We have since made more progress on those problems than I had dared even dream. Our success in protecting and restoring wildness has given me hope and confidence, a big change from where I began as a hard-edged misanthropic revolutionary for nature.

From my front-row observation point, I can assess what has worked best not only for nature, but also for the larger social context of a stable society. I have witnessed reactionary organizers and politicians rise and fall, community sentiments evolve, and America go through several shocking fits of populism. I am convinced that conservation progress cannot be fully measured or achieved apart from the health of our democracy and the well-being of our communities, including rural ones.

I have observed much about people, nature, politics, and strategy. This book shares some of those experiences and lessons in the hope of a better future. At twenty-two, I was a radical protest leader, dabbling in eco-sabotage. At sixty-two, I lead efforts that address big conservation challenges through collaboration, eschewing political polarization. The path between took turns worth recounting. But first a bit more about my life, and the events and experiences that led me to be a nature warrior and equipped me to succeed.

2

Roots and Sprouting

The author being arrested at a forest protest in 1988
(photo courtesy of Archives & Special Collections, Western Libraries,
Western Washington University – Fishtown0102a)

I grew up the youngest of four in Deerfield, Illinois, in Chicago's northern burbs. I played average football for Highland Park High School but was a state medalist in the pole vault. I was an inattentive student in everything except shop classes (wood, metal, auto) and the natural sciences. When I headed off to Montana State University in 1981, obliviously enrolled to study wildlife management, it was mostly to continue pole vaulting.

My family history is a common one of eastern European Jewish migration to Chicago. The great grandparents of my father, Ira, came from Lithuania in the late-nineteenth century, as antisemitism was rising across Europe. I was named Mitchell in honor of a reputed mensch, Moses Salk, the grandfather of my paternal grandmother, Gladys. Moses ran a necktie factory in Chicago and employed there a continuous flow of relatives from the Old Country. Dad described Moses's apartment as being full of couch-surfing immigrants. Dad's father, Harry Friedman, entered the University of Chicago at age sixteen, paying his way with a job at Walgreens, and became a prominent Chicago physician. Dad put himself through law school by selling hot dogs at Wrigley Field. He then enlisted as an officer in the U.S. Navy, delaying his law career. By the time I came along, he was in a small firm, a partnership with an already-accomplished attorney who focused on pro bono legal work for Indian tribes. One of my earliest memories is accompanying Dad as he delivered bags of groceries to a gymnasium where Indian activists, probably with the American Indian Movement, were camped.

I would not describe either of my parents as having been activists at any point, but each surely had a strong social conscience and dabbled in causes. My oldest brother Ross had the idea to video each now-elderly parent in a sort of oral history while we were all gathered for Thanksgiving one year. I was surprised to learn that, among other things, Mom had been in the streets during the infamous 1968 Democratic Convention in Chicago.

My mother was Francine Hirsch. Her mother, who passed before my arrival, was born around the turn of the century in England as her family migrated from Odessa, Ukraine. Mom's father, Victor, and his older brother came as barefoot kids from Hungary to reunite with their mother, who had gone ahead to Chicago. Her new husband didn't want them around, so they were sent to a Jewish boys' home, from which they eventually ran away. They lied about their age to join the Navy, where Vic took up boxing when somebody noticed how effectively he fought off antisemitic bullies. He became the Navy champ in his weight class and went on to a successful prize fighting career that he leveraged into ownership of a Chicago nightclub during the city's mob heyday. Actually, while Mom referred to it as a "club," the Prohibition-era timing means it must have been a speakeasy. We were told that he paid protection money to the likes of Al Capone. He lost everything in the market crash that set off the Great Depression. Jobless, he then became active in the Freemasons for the initial reason that doing so gave his family access to the soup kitchen they operated. I inherited his Masonic ring and tie clip, which I wear on family occasions.

My parents grew up in the shadow of the Holocaust and took Judaism seriously, even if they were not particularly spiritual. Their observance fell flat with me, though I did become bar mitzvah. My personal cosmology had nature as the higher power that gave meaning to life. Notions of an omnipotent God have always struck me as far-fetched. I remember eight-year-old me arguing with a Hebrew school teacher against the existence of God.

My bedroom was adorned with centerfold posters of wildlife from Cousteau Society newsletters, my membership having been a gift from Ross. My passion for nature and wilderness was nourished in my early teens by weeks-long YMCA excursions into the Boundary Waters Canoe Area Wilderness of northern Minnesota. A poignant memory has me alone, the only early riser in our shoreline camp, as a mist lay over the tranquil little lake. In that mist stood a bull moose, knee-deep in the shallows like an ethereal demigod. I was hooked.

How hooked? Here is an example that my buddy Marty Coyne will not let me live down. Marty was an Army kid from nearby Fort Sheridan. We drove to Great Smoky Mountains National Park for Spring Break of our Junior year. On a particular trail, Marty was lost in his nature bliss, whistling as he trekked. But my bliss required silence to better hear nature, and I demanded he shut up. You may be familiar with the type—that was me.

My youth jobs were varied, including pumping gas at Joe's Standard and Mac's Standard, painting house exteriors, and stocking shelves at Mutual Hardware. I drove a forklift in an Evanston, Illinois plastics factory owned by the family of my new stepfather (my parents split during my early teens), where I was the lone white guy on the floor. Chicago police daringly raided me and five black coworkers as we shared an after-work sixpack in a lakeshore park. That was my first night in jail.

For my final high school summer, I (with Dad's help) landed work as a ranch hand. I drove my beater red Chevy Impala west to the Ferguson Ranch outside Cheyenne, Wyoming. Its long washboard gravel approach rattled off my rearview mirror. My job was to help Dick, the patriarch and third generation of a pioneer family, and Ed, the tall and lanky fourth generation, run Black Angus cattle on ten thousand acres of semi-arid hill country with patches of pines. I made three hundred fifty dollars per month, slept alone in an old bunkhouse that once billeted eight working men, and used my fake Illinois ID to drink beer at a topless bar called the Green Door. Every morning began with Gladys Ferguson serving Dick and me each a giant breakfast: two eggs, bacon, a bowl of Kellogg's All-Bran cereal, and a big Krusteaz pancake, two if I was particularly hungry. Lunch was often either roast beef and potatoes or, if we could not be home, something hearty in a thermos. Then roast beef for dinner.

It was a hot summer, with some days topping one hundred degrees. Standard cowboy attire was boots with pointy toes (for stirrups) and flat soles (for cow shit), jeans and long-sleeved shirt (defense against deer flies and horse flies), leather gloves, and a Stetson hat (for sun and rain).

Late on a particularly long day during which we had driven cattle since sunrise, I was sweaty and bushed in the saddle. The cows trudged along, driven by the nips of Queensland blue heelers, dogs so tough that one will get kicked through the air, land in a roll, then bolt back to that same cow heel. We rode out of a long draw in which the air was oppressively still, emerging to a cool breeze blowing from distant high country.

Gazing at the snow-topped mountains, I remarked to Ed, "That's beautiful, isn't it?"

"I'm a cattleman," he replied. "What's beautiful to me is grass."

What I took from that comment was worth more than the three hundred fifty bucks per month. It was an early introduction into the variability of perspective that would influence so much of my later work.

I spent another summer in Savage, Montana, with its two bars and a post office, as a per-diem volunteer to the Montana

Department of Fish, Wildlife and Parks, assisting a graduate student studying white-tailed deer that spent nights grazing in fields of sugar beets aside the Yellowstone River. We lived in a little house owned by the agency and fed on accumulated game meat from the freezer, plus catfish and such we caught using setlines baited with rotted venison.

Had I enrolled at MSU a decade later, I probably would still be in Bozeman. But in its pre-glamour days of the early 1980s, it didn't quite hold my interest. I had washed out of pole vaulting, didn't connect with the women (my fault, not theirs), and, despite straight As, had concluded that wildlife management was not for me, as management itself was contrary to the wild nature I sought. I treaded water my sophomore year with classes in classic literature and Eastern philosophy, trying to make sense of the world.

I left Bozeman for home, where I spent a summer as a framing carpenter and grunt for my brother, a budding homebuilder, before heading off to New England for a maritime program. SEA Semester entailed six dry weeks of lectures in Woods Hole, Massachusetts, followed by six sweet weeks sailing a 125-foot staysail schooner across the Caribbean while studying oceanography. I did nifty research on coral reef ecology in a bay of Tobago, where I observed and measured fish distribution governed by the algae grazing of black spiny sea urchins, themselves limited by wave intensity correlated to water depth. I loved the experience, but I fit in no better on the East Coast—which I considered to be something like the Old World—than I had in Highland Park or Bozeman. So, next was Seattle and the University of Washington, where I hoped to get a degree, any degree, while checking out the Northwest. Here, I found my place.

Luck found me on my first day at UW. I was perusing the curriculum book when I noticed a section called environmental studies. I had never heard of that. I wandered over to the little annex that housed the program and was greeted by Polly Dyer, an emphatic conservation luminary who worked there in administration. At her urging, I made environmental studies a minor to a zoology major.

My two years at UW were full. I could hardly have gotten a better education—studying under world-class ecologists like Bob Paine and Gordon Orians. The environmental studies track delivered interdisciplinary courses, such as environmental law with Alan Merson, which somehow anticipated what would later serve me well in a life committed to conservation advocacy.

I fell in with activism. As a new friend, Victor Garcia, and I walked out of a lecture hall in the April of '85, we noticed a flyer on the wall: *Earth First! Meeting Tonight*. What was that? We attended. George Draffan hosted the meeting. He had just started UW graduate studies in library science, moving up from Eugene, Oregon, where he had been active in Earth First! George called the meeting mostly to meet like-minded people. It worked. I was already familiar with the books of Edward Abbey, including *The Monkey Wrench Gang*, that informed the movement's culture. I fell right in, making commitments that my Jewish sense of responsibility required that I keep.

My first task was to organize a little observation at UW for the event of Earth Day, which was then just a week or so away. It was a pathetic thing, with me having conned a professor or two to stand outside the student union building at lunchtime, in the rain, lecturing to disinterested passersby. But it was a start.

George had also tasked me with tracking notices of timber sales on the nearby Mt. Baker-Snoqualmie National Forest. It was all Greek to me at the beginning, but it seemed important. It would not be until the next year, 1986, when scientists would publish the first research paper that defined old-growth forests in the western Pacific Northwest, and countless books on the subject were yet to come. But the notion that there was extraordinary value in primeval forest was intuitively obvious, especially considering the grandeur of the trees. Forests of big, old trees play important ecological functions, including providing habitats for species that do not thrive elsewhere. The northern spotted owl is an illustrious example. In 1985, the U.S. Forest Service was logging ancient forest at a fevered pace, and biologists had just brought to light the danger to spotted owls. It was a bona fide ecological emergency.

Tree-sitting in the Millenium Grove was my first act of civil disobedience. I recall the reaction of my family being a bit mixed, maybe intrigued but with some trepidation. My brother Rick sent me a thoughtful and encouraging short note, which struck me as altogether novel. The next summer, 1986, I organized and got arrested in Washington State's first protest of logging ancient forests.

The background to that protest involved the Forest Service having sold rights to log the Swauk Meadow timber sale, near Blewett Pass, an hour west of Wenatchee. A spotted owl nest was then discovered within an area slated to be logged, prompting an administrative challenge by the Audubon Society and the Washington Department of Game (as it was then called). The Forest Service promised to delay logging until after the appeal was resolved. Experience had taught us not to trust such promises. We informed news media that Earth First! would be protesting the next day at the Forest Service office in the town of Cle Elum. A group of us decided to spend that night camped out in the timber sale area. We sat up late around a campfire, preparing for the ordeal ahead, then retired to sleeping bags. As we lay awake, we heard the calls of a spotted owl. Hoo hoo-hoo hoooooo. She was somewhere in the trees close to us. We fell asleep to the sound of her calls and awoke hours later in a panic to the morning buzz of chainsaws. The Forest Service had lied; logging had commenced.

George and I bolted in his old pickup truck for the nearest pay phone, half an hour away. From there, we called down our list of press contacts, breathlessly informing them of a change in plans. Instead of guerrilla theater in an office, there would be a confrontation in the woods. We returned in time to see a KING5 TV helicopter flying in a news crew from Seattle, and for me to join five friends sitting on the gravel logging road, blockading access. We were soon arrested and carried off in squad cars to Kittitas County jail, which, as county jails go, was pretty nice. My friend Rhys Roth and I had our own cell, where we amused ourselves with floor games like football using a triangle of folded paper. A third member of our group, Larry, was separated into his own cell. With his more nervous disposition, Larry was having a rough time and frequently complained. The three women were in a different cell block.

By 1989, I had also been jailed in Whatcom, Skagit, and Okanogan counties of Washington, Benton and Josephine counties in Oregon, and a small jail in Mammoth, Wyoming. The latter was for protesting the planned expansion of a Yellowstone campground in grizzly bear habitat. Protests in which I wasn't jailed include the Grand Canyon (something about uranium), Tofino, British Columbia (ancient forest), and the University of Washington (South African apartheid). There was also a night in Bozeman's drunk tank for which I can't claim any lofty cause. I may be forgetting others, but I kept no journal.

We called protests *direct actions*, not just in Earth First! but across activist movements. My dad hated the term, which reminded him of *aktion*, a euphemism Nazis used for mass murder operations.

The most dramatic situation might have been one involving a Forest Service logging show in the valley of Illabot Creek, in northwest Washington's Skagit County in 1987. The ancient forest war was in full swing by this time, with tension in logging towns understandably sky-high. The urgency that I and people like me felt about saving ancient forests and, via their proxy, nature at large, was probably no greater than that felt by those whose livelihoods, identities, and family well-being were at stake. We had their full attention.

Our base camp during a week of protests was in a campground near the town of Marblemount. A couple of people came into camp one night to warn us that there was bar talk of a group mustering to come crack heads. None came, for reasons I don't know. We put our own bodies on the line the final day with how we chose to block the logging road on which semi-trucks hauled timber to a sawmill.

Our objective was to stage an image for press cameras in which we would block a truck laden with giant logs. That involved stopping at a precise spot a fully loaded semi running downhill. We picked our location, downhill of a curve and with a spur road entering just above us. Victor Garcia took his old Toyota truck up the road a quarter-mile and parked on the shoulder. When he heard the approach of a loaded log truck, he pulled out in front of it and progressively slowed, taking the truck through downshifts to a safer speed, then ducked off onto the spur road. A group of us were standing in the road as the truck, now on its own, approached. It was still going a bit too fast, the driver being perhaps inclined to play chicken with us. I called out, "now!" for us all to turn, putting our backs to the truck. Still, it came on too fast. I shouted, "sit!" and we sat. He stopped with his hot grill at our necks. If I were smarter, I would have been more terrified than exhilarated. I really should have been. But I was on a mission.

I would not say that my mission was protecting ancient forests. I had deeper passions for wildlife and whole ecosystems. At that time, coral reefs held more intrigue for me than Northwest old-growth forests. But for a young man determined to intervene in industrial humanity's destruction of wild Earth, I could sure have done worse than to happen into the ancient forest war. As a proxy for global biodiversity, it stood in just fine. I was energized, proud, and yes, empowered.

Press coverage and recognition were excellent, and I was feeling like a bigshot with attending swagger. Women noticed. Even my luminary UW professors quietly supported my extracurriculars.

After graduating, I moved to Bellingham, Washington. I afforded my cheap activist lifestyle by working periodic stints of two or three months in the North Pacific or Bering Sea, where I monitored fish hauls on various Japanese, Korean, and Polish trawlers and longliners.

I wish I could remember everyone who I agitated amongst and got arrested with, but there are a few who particularly come to mind. Some I remain close with. Some even still call me Budworm, harkening back to my old arboreal pseudonym. George, who I mentioned previously, was my mentor and a master researcher. He filled our newsletters with original information about timber corporations but stayed as far as he could from the police. Rhys, who is the son of a hippie farmer outside Seattle, has dedicated his life to fighting climate change. Victor grew up on the Washington Coast and, like me, worked in the Alaska fisheries. He went on to be a celebrated biology teacher at Anacortes High School. Greg Wingard looked scruffy with his long hair and beard hanging down over a ragged T-shirt. But he was (and is) a savant in environmental remediation. Greg was an everyman who liked to converse with police officers as they arrested and processed us. "The cops are our friends" became his catchphrase. Beth was my girlfriend and had grown up outside Seattle. I don't remember her mother expressing any anger at me for her activism. Charley Knox is an Army combat medic veteran who had deployed in the Dominican Republic in the 1960s, after which he returned traumatized and radicalized to his home state of Washington. He provided logistical support and amusement but shared George's disinclination for any involvement with the police. David Helm, originally from Ohio, is like Charley in that he is twenty years my senior and a veteran, in his case of the Navy during Vietnam. David is a jack-of-all-trades and especially gifted with wood. He never hesitated to get arrested.

In June of 1987, David, a Colorado woman named Kate, and I locked ourselves between the two sets of double doors in the entryway of the Siskiyou National Forest's headquarters in Grants Pass, Oregon. The police had to bring in the Fire Department to cut us out, using a special tool that was like a circular saw. That earned us a sentence of two weeks, to be served immediately. I was welcomed in the jail by a man who was doing real time for serious crimes, including, I believe, murder. He had seen us on the TV news and was impressed enough to spread word to the White Supremacists and other hardcore types that we were not to be harassed. My time there was uneventful, boring if I remember right.

For this Midwest transplant in my early twenties, I had gotten myself solidly onto what felt like a righteous nature-saving path. I was living my best life and would probably do it all again, or at least most of it.

Before we move on, I need to recount a less noble event. In the fall of 1985, after my first Alaska stint, I returned to Corvallis to see the stumps of Millenium Grove. Also visiting was a journalist who was assigned to cover Earth First! for a national magazine. She was somewhat interested in tree-sitting, but really wanted to tag along on a monkeywrenching foray. I thought it was a bad idea, but Mikal acquiesced. The journalist got more than she bargained for!

The four of us—Mikal (Doug Fir), Val (Rhoda Dendron), the writer, and I—went out that night in dark clothes. Our hooligan mission was to cut down a billboard. I recall that Mikal's previous antics had left standing only one billboard in Corvallis that had the kind of wooden posts we would be able to cut through. It advertised cigarettes, which I will grasp as added justification for its demise. We did most things right: parking far from the scene, finding our way to the billboard, felling it with bowsaws and ropes, and making our escape. Just one mistake—the route Mikal led back to the car took us unknowingly past the fuel pound where Corvallis Police officers filled their patrol vehicles. We were four camouflaged knuckleheads carrying ropes and saws, slinking suspiciously in front of the cops. They held us until they could figure out what crime we had committed.

3

From Radical Action to Radical Impact

Dana Lyons on The Big One
(photo by the author)

"Hold off on that until I get back," I said to Mikal as I left Bellingham early in 1988 for another round in the Bering Sea.

Mikal's feverish mind had generated its millionth idea: We should produce an Earth First! proposal for a vast protected wilderness in the North Cascades Ecosystem.

The *Earth First! Journal* sometimes featured proposals for sweeping protections of wild, rugged landscapes. This was a significant but overlooked aspect of Earth First!, better known for the provocative field tactics of civil disobedience and monkeywrenching. The movement also included an artistic wing that created poetry and songs meant to entertain the ranks and incubate a new relationship with nature. That biocentric culture never caught on at scale. But conservation of large landscape ecosystems has, and perhaps those Earth First! proposals played a role. Mikal's idea was to try that for the North Cascades, the stunning mountain range visible from Bellingham.

The idea had instant resonance for me, with my education in ecology. A singular lecture in a 400-level class made a big impression. Dr. Orians had described important new concepts in ecology. The viability of a wildlife population varies with its size, which is in turn related to the extent of its habitat. Patches of habitat behave like islands in the sea, with the ability of resident species to persist, increasing with both the size of a patch and its proximity to additional patches. If there are corridors linking patches together (like bridges linking islands), the habitat is additive and can support larger populations and therefore more species. This stuff became core to an emerging scientific discipline called conservation biology.

Mikal's idea was for a giant protected area to be free of industrial extraction. It catalyzed in me a chance to apply these new scientific concepts to a practical objective: the design of, and justification for, a bold land conservation initiative. Also, as I mentioned, protecting whole ecosystems and their iconic wildlife is much closer to my core passion than forests, even ancient ones. The North Cascades had a head start toward this goal, as conservation campaigns from the mid-1960s to 1984 had already won from Congress a national park and numerous protected wilderness areas. I acted on Mikal's idea by producing a book when I returned from Alaska a couple months later. I wrote parts and organized contributions from knowledgeable friends. I "published" it at a local copy shop, printing a few hundred copies of *Forever Wild: Conserving the Greater North Cascades Ecosystem*. The heart of the book was a chapter applying new research findings to calculate how much of the North Cascades should be protected to sustain a viable population of grizzly bears. I dedicated the book to my newborn niece, the first of a new generation in my family.

Forever Wild was surprisingly well received. A division within the Washington Department of Game offered me a grant of a few hundred bucks to print more copies. (A few years later, we published a more formal version, *Cascadia Wild: Protecting an International Ecosystem*, that contained more scholarly contributions, including one from Dr. Reed Noss, an international leader in conservation biology.) As I wrote in the Washington Earth First! newsletter in the spring of 1989, "When we published *Forever Wild* last year, we couldn't guess the reaction. The book has really struck home with a lot of people. . . . There is a dire need in Washington for a conservation biology-advocacy/education group. I feel the call to fill that niche."

Around this time, I was invited to join the board of Bellingham's local chapter of the Audubon Society. I thought they were nuts in wanting to associate with me, a branded rabble-rouser. I accepted the invitation, giggling to myself that this was an opportunity to radicalize little old ladies. I quickly learned that the little old ladies needed no radicalization, already fully sharing my love of, and commitment to, wild nature. The distinction was only in how they pursued their objectives. This experience, combined with the encouraging response to my book and its big ideas, got me questioning my own actions. If people are already inclined to love nature and to support its protection, is radical or confrontational protest really the best way to invite and build their engagement?

I incorporated a new organization as an outlet to pursue the heart of *Forever Wild*, which was science-based conservation of the North Cascades Ecosystem and the broader Northwest landscape. We have called the organization Conservation Northwest (CNW) for the last twenty years, though its founding name was Greater Ecosystem Alliance. I spent the following decades fulfilling the vision of *Forever Wild*. I will recount some of that, but not just yet. First comes another big idea I had that year.

By late 1988, I felt that the movement to protect ancient forests had reached a new phase. Powerful national organizations had joined the battle, leading me to think that getting arrested was no longer the best use of my time and talents. I wanted to help build national awareness and power to enable government action to protect the forests. I had also become increasingly turned off to escalating tactics. I remember watching Mikal stand outside the window of a cafeteria in which Forest Service employees were taking their lunch, menacingly poking needles into a doll-sized Smokey Bear. I had myself just dumped a bucket of sawdust in the reception area of that office. It was childishly amusing at the time, but some of the workers were disturbed enough by the action to need counseling.

In another infamous protest that summer, hundreds of us Earth First!ers swarmed the headquarters of the Okanogan National Forest. We were there to protest the logging of high-elevation forests that provide habitat for lynx and other carnivores. But since the logging was shut down for summer wildfire season, we adapted by moving the protest to town. Big mistake! From the roof of the building, I watched autonomous teams carry out their own creative attacks, from mild (chalk art) to monstrous (tampering with the building's electrical box), as riot police and snarling German shepherds tried to gain control. I was hardly innocent. Not only did I instigate the whole episode, but I carried a cow pie onto that roof, where I rubbed it into the air intake of the building's air conditioner. That caused enough stink inside the office to force them to go without AC on that sweltering day. I had succeeded in offending even myself. It was clear that I was no longer a good fit for the group I led.

That December, I announced to my friends that I was leaving Earth First! I also unveiled my next project, proposing the far-fetched scheme to obtain a giant log and a semi-truck to carry it around America. I invited help. The following spring of 1989, we launched the Ancient Forest Rescue Expedition. This is how I explained both the political context and my idea in the Washington Earth First! newsletter: ". . . we might soon expect a legal injunction on old-growth/spotted owl habitat logging. . . . The (Rescue) Expedition's mission is to build support enough to withstand a political backlash, at the same time creating a network ready to support our forest conservation legislative proposal. If we fail, Congress will most likely either exempt the spotted owl from the Endangered Species Act or bargain a deal. . . . Frankly, I'm scared. And if I didn't have the hope of the Expedition, callouses would surely thicken my sledgin' right hand."

That reference at the end is to tree spiking, and it was bluster. I have no doubt that tree spiking was spreading in Washington. The sheriff of Okanogan County, Jim Weed, had told *Loggers World Magazine* of at least twenty-two incidents of spikes hitting mill equipment in his county in just the first six months of 1988. (The single time that I spiked trees was in Skagit County, and they never ran through a mill, as they remain standing today.) At the national level, things were even hotter. The FBI had infiltrated an Earth First! group in the American Southwest and, in May of 1989, arrested four people for conspiring to sabotage power lines leading to nuclear power stations. My decision to go mainstream was timely.

This was an important transition in my life, so I want to explain it, to the extent that my memory allows. I left Earth First! when things were really heating up and I had two different reasons for doing so. One was that I saw the opportunity to have more strategic impact through other means. My friends and I had gotten arrested enough, and the impact was diminishing. Protesting had served its purpose. I had the skills and ideas to try something new and felt moved to do so. I think you will see that decision vindicated as my story proceeds.

The second reason was that I had become turned off by some of what I was observing in Earth First! I must take responsibility for some of the actions that offended me, as I had pushed the envelope as a leader. But others were pushing that envelope, too, in ways that did not sit well with me. If I had not had the sense to back off a bit before things got too ugly for my liking, at least I had the sense to feel when we had gone too far. I was ready for change. The Ancient Forest Rescue Expedition provided the perfect transition in my life and activism.

The Rescue Expedition launched with Seattle events around Earth Day of 1989. Over twenty-nine days we visited twenty-eight states with our seven-foot-wide, twenty-foot-long Douglas fir log named the Big One. To its rear end we had stapled laminated labels of historic events corresponding to the Big One's 731 tree rings, noting for instance the American Revolution, the sailing of Columbus, and, on a subsequent tour with an even older log, the drafting of the Magna Carta.

I planned our route to visit major media hubs and the districts of key members of Congress. Our visits were hosted by local groups I had recruited and prepped in advance, such as chapters of the Audubon Society and Sierra Club and, in Chicago, my big sister, Marcia. Hosts arranged logistics, invited attendees to our press conferences, and prepared evening events of a slideshow, music, and speeches. They also gave floor space for the sleeping bags of our ample crew, which included a truck driver, musician, and at least one experienced forest campaigner with speaking skills. The tour generated great press coverage, as passionate activists with a giant log had irresistible novelty. We organized constituent mail to Congress and compiled lists of people to stay in touch with.

By ironic coincidence, we were in Bismarck, North Dakota while President George H. W. Bush was there to plant a tree for Earth Day. This was a bit awkward for our hosts who worked for a state agency and had to talk me out of embarrassing the President of the United States in their hometown.

In the deep South, we were surprised at how the Big One evoked emotion from those who remembered their own erstwhile big trees, mostly lost by then to plantations of young pines to be ground into pulp for paper products. "Now there aren't even squirrels living there" was a lament I heard more than once. I recall truck drivers racing after us on foot, not wanting to lose the emotional connection they had made with our log during breaks in rest areas. Many people, young and old, cried to learn the story of our tree and those like it. While there's a certain sanctimonious buzz to getting arrested with six hippies for a good cause, this mainstream roadshow generated further proof that, like with the little old ladies of Audubon in Bellingham, lovers of nature are not an exclusive club.

In Washington, D.C., we circled the Capitol, blasting the truck's horn. We thought that was power. Then we got the bright idea to just enter the halls of Congress. In jeans and T-shirts, Ric Bailey (a unique combination of professional trucker and forest campaigner) and I visited congressional offices to tell our story and show photos of majestic ancient forests and their remains. Through this, I experienced the direct power we citizens have in the accessibility of our government. I have since made countless lobbying trips there.

The Expedition helped teach me perseverance. I had no choice, as problems constantly had to be overcome. Like the time our donated VW van (we couldn't fit all our people and gear in the cab of the semi) died before reaching the gig, and then I accidentally spilled all the slides from the carousel ten minutes before showtime. I remember midway through the month-long journey when a shortage of donations gave me financial panic. Lou Gold, the sage of Oregon's Bald Mountain, had to instruct me to not only have faith but to not dare try rationing the crew's food. Our second tour, the next year, was a ten-week odyssey that required me to rotate crew in shifts. One Oregon activist told me he could drive a semi. Turned out he had only driven buses. Within his first quarter-mile at the wheel, the difference became clear, as he could not complete a gear shift. I had to scramble to get Peter Hirsh, the world's most soulful truck driver who we had found through a classified ad, to scurry to whatever state the log was mired in and salvage the show.

Sadly, a similar effort today would have far less impact. American media has changed. In many small towns, there is no longer a local paper or a spare news photographer to report on a spectacle like an out-of-town log. Online clicks also demand that news stories use conflict to trigger emotion. Likewise, Congress has changed, as has my experience as a citizen lobbyist. Big money and polarization have reduced the influence of the common citizen. But in our original timing, we had real impact. I maintain hope that in due time, with changes in Congress and the Supreme Court, truer democracy will be restored.

How did we get a giant log? Deception. A couple of our quirkier team members visited sawmills on the Olympic Peninsula, misrepresenting themselves as purchasing a log for Native American carvers. We got lucky with a small mill called Owl Lumber that had an iconoclastic and politically progressive owner, who later became a supporter and friend. We didn't risk informing him of our true purpose until the show was on the road and the Big One safely out of state.

How did we pay for it? Don't tell the IRS, but it all went through my personal checking account. It cost about $10,000 to acquire the log, lease and fuel the truck, print T-shirts, and feed the crew. We raised about that same amount through donations and sales of swag, plus what I made by selling the processed remains of the Big One, which I foolishly had milled. The project proved popular enough that I organized two more tours, requiring us to buy two additional logs, as after each exhausting, harrowing experience, I swore it would be the last.

I had grown in my empowerment. I had a lot of cachet as a protest leader, showing the ability to muster crowds, command a confrontational situation, and garner press. That is heady stuff for a young man. But in walking away from those tactics, I found that my science education, flair for spectacle, and organizing and leadership skills opened ways to be more effective with an American populace that to a great degree shared my love of nature. I was learning strategy and was hungry to know more.

I prowled used bookstores for tattered activist manuals like Saul Alinsky's *Rules for Radicals* and the Sierra Club's *Ecotactics*, but these left me unfulfilled. Martial books like Sun Tzu's *The Art of War* and Miyamoto Musashi's *The Book of Five Rings* were fascinating but difficult to apply to my situation. Captain Paul Watson, leader of the Sea Shepherd Society, had written *Earthforce!* to translate Sun Tzu's war principles to conservation campaigns, but that too fell short of what I was looking for. I therefore went deep into military history. I believe it was in John Keegan's *A History of Warfare* where I read that in war, as in life, an indirect approach is often best. That was the nugget I had been searching for! The long way around can be the shortest. Hannibal brought his army over the Alps to surprise Rome from behind. George Washington crossed the Delaware River on a winter night to catch the Hessians off-guard. This simple principle made me think of people I knew who had a soft and circuitous touch for persuasion, which can be annoying for a Type A personality like me but is observably effective. Success in conflict is affected not just by maximizing one's own power but also by minimizing the resistance of the ostensible adversary. Perhaps indirect approaches might enable one to protect nature with less conflict. It took me years to find ways to test this idea, but it proved out.

4

Learning from Success and Failure

Old-growth forest in Whatcom County, WA
(photo courtesy of Conservation Northwest)

I was standing backstage with Carole King. Yes, that Carole King—revered singer/songwriter who moonlights as a conservationist. We were watching Neil Young play "After the Gold Rush" ("mother nature on the run . . .") on what I recall was a giant organ. Behind Neil, from our vantage, was Portland's Waterfront Park overflowing with seventy thousand people enduring cold spring rain. President Bill Clinton circled overhead on Air Force One with much of his cabinet onboard. Overcome with emotion even now, for the hundredth time as I write this, I began to cry.

"We did it, Carole," I said. "We've saved the ancient forests."

This was April 1, 1993, the first year of Clinton's presidency. The following day, he would host in the Portland Convention Center his Forest Conference, a roundtable of invitees to share perspectives on the problems (ecological and social) and solutions in the woods. In a span of eight years, we had caused the ancient forest issue to elevate from a few radicals protesting in the woods to a national issue high on the agenda of a new president who had made campaign promises to resolve the conflict.

I had spent the preceding two weeks in Portland, scrambling with a handful of other activists and some professionals funded by The Bullitt Foundation to organize an event worthy of the moment. We did our job well, drawing a huge crowd to hear speeches and a slate of famous performers. On the big day itself, I had the job of escorting celebrities to the media tent for interviews. It also fell to me to quell a small protest from three misguided Earth First!ers who felt the message should be more about activists than forests.

The result of the Forest Conference was Clinton directing a panel of four top scientists, led by the venerable Dr. Jerry Franklin, to develop options for new policy. A year later, they presented those options, and the result was Clinton establishing the Northwest Forest Plan. The plan stands to this day as perhaps the world's foremost science-driven, regional-scale plan for conserving a lucrative resource. It put in place a set of forest reserves (mostly based on spotted owl habitat needs) on federal lands across the region, inside of which the only logging allowed is for ecological objective. It also established protections for trees buffering streams. This drastically reduced the amount of old forest available to be cut and, therefore, greatly reduced logging of federal public forest. At the start of my forest activism, in 1985, the U.S. Forest Service was facilitating the clearcutting of two square miles per week of classic ancient forests in western Washington and Oregon. Protests and litigation converted this ecological crisis into a political one, which Clinton's 1994 Northwest Forest Plan resolved by protecting millions of acres of old forest. It remains in effect today. Work to protect old forests wasn't quite finished, as you'll see in the pages ahead. Still, in the thirty years since, we have lost a net of less than two percent of the amount of old-growth forest that stood then on federal lands in the region covered by the plan (generally the range of the northern spotted owl, which includes northern California). Most of that loss was from wildfire, with only about ten thousand acres lost to logging. Meanwhile, moderately old forests continue to grow into ancient forests, so the net amount of old-growth forest will improve unless logging policies or fire trends drastically change. This ecosystem is of great value in storing carbon, filtering water into clear-running streams, and sustaining biodiversity. Whether it will harbor long its spotted owls is tenuous, mostly due to competition from barred owls, a larger and more aggressive and adaptable cousin of spotteds that have in recent decades spread across the region.

The monumental advance that was the Northwest Forest Plan came from the combined effort of many scientists, activists, lawyers, lobbyists, and others. My involvement was impactful in a couple ways. First, my role in protests and in driving a log around the country helped raise public attention to the majesty of iconic, big, old trees. But my team and I were also building awareness (through articles, brochures, and conferences) of how those trees were part of a larger ecosystem, and the importance of that to the emergent concept of biodiversity. The emotional surge I get whenever I hear "After the Gold Rush" is pride from knowing that I did my part and that our collective accomplishment was at a historic scale.

The Clinton years, however, were not all glory. While the elections of 1992 were a sweep for Democrats, bringing to office Clinton and congressional majorities, the pendulum swung back hard in 1994. Republicans won a majority in the House for the first time in a generation behind the cynical leadership of Newt Gingrich and his so-called Contract with America, which seeded the brand of Republican populism that still manifests today in Donald Trump. That was a strange time, watching the conservative backlash to Clinton build at a local level.

At the time, CNW's feature campaign was to win designation of an international park in the North Cascades. This was my idea for achieving goals from my book, *Forever Wild*, by protecting remaining wild areas on both sides of the border and instituting transborder cooperation for ecosystem conservation. In my naïve mind, the medicine was ecological protection, while the spoonful of sugar was the label of international park. I had company in that delusion with partners including The Bullitt Foundation,

National Parks and Conservation Association, the Wilderness Society, North Cascades Conservation Council, and Western Canada Wilderness Committee. We were a formidable coalition. But the opposition was different than we could have imagined.

One day, an aide to Mike Lowry, the governor of Washington, told me that he had gotten a call from a small city on the eastern margin of the North Cascades. "The guy told me that he heard that Canadian or UN tanks had just rolled through town. I asked him whether he could see where the tank tracks had deeply rutted the road pavement. He said no, so I told him there were no tanks and he should relax."

Parts of America had seemed to lose their minds. In rural areas across the country, but mostly near the Canadian border, people reported seeing black helicopters and blue-helmeted soldiers of the United Nations. People were forming themselves into militias, or at least hopped-up militant groups with militia in their names. They feared America was being taken over by a "new world order," and they were ready to defend their country from this change, whatever it might be. It wasn't solely a reaction to Clinton, who they characterized as a liberal agent of foreign powers, but also of his predecessor, Republican George H. W. Bush, who was first to use the phrase "new world order."

In Washington, it manifested as a grassroots backlash against my innocent international park proposal. It didn't help that we had wantonly called ourselves the Cascades International Alliance, or CIA. Oops! A magazine called *Executive Intelligence Review*, associated with conspiracist Lyndon LaRouche, portrayed us as dupes of the British House of Windsor: "Fulfilling a longstanding British Crown policy, efforts are under way to 'balkanize' North and South America into autonomous zones that would destroy the sovereignty of every nation. . . . One of the most advanced schemes, 'Cascadia' . . . would be off-limits to all human beings."

People I had never heard of were guest speakers in standing room-only meetings held in rural foothill towns. One such speaker, Don Kehoe, was quoted as saying to a meeting in Mount Vernon, Washington that, "This park calls for the first physical breakup of the United States. It will eliminate borders. It will destroy the free and constitutional Republic of the United States of America." That was quite an exaggeration from the improved stewardship of wildlife habitat that we'd proposed!

I attended one of those meetings in an old grange hall not far from Bellingham. I brought a few friends, but we were outnumbered by about two hundred hostile attendees. There were whispered threats and demonstrations of sleeves being rolled up. One featured speaker was Chuck Cushman, a well-known leader of a reactionary movement opposing environmental measures. The first time I met Chuck, he said, "Woohoo, one of the great ones!" and we formed an amiable cat-and-mouse relationship. After I managed to get access to the stage for a short speech to the surly crowd, assuring them that I too was a father and paid payroll and taxes, Chuck kindly escorted me and my friends to our cars. I think the pitchfork-and-torches feel of these crowds was disconcerting even to an experienced agitator like Chuck.

Our international park proposal died a quiet death, run over by this train that none had seen coming. The same dynamic played out in Congress, as Gingrich and his revolutionaries upended congressional decorum and pursued their extreme agenda, including attacks on environmental laws, owning Clinton until they overplayed their hand by causing a government shutdown.

One of the laws passed in this period was colloquially known as the "clearcut rider." In legislation, a rider is a short amendment added to a must-pass spending bill to which it is not germane. We had seen these before, as this was how powerful timber-favoring congressmen from Washington and Oregon were able to override green judicial rulings. They would simply add language to a big spending bill, stating that, "Notwithstanding any provision of law, the Secretary shall" get a bunch of ancient forest cut down.

Despite the public support we had built, and the body of science that Clinton's process and Northwest Forest Plan had brought to bear, Senator Slade Gorton (R, WA) and Representative Norm Dicks (D, WA) attached an amendment to a 1995 spending bill that Clinton could not afford to veto. Though we did ask. A donor paid my way to attend a Clinton fundraiser in Seattle's ritzy Rainier Club. I waited in a long line for my chance to pose for a photo with the president. As we shook hands, I mumbled one of the craziest things I have ever said: "Mr. President, I think you should veto that Oklahoma City relief bill." In his Arkansas drawl, he replied, "Why, because of the logging rider?" And he proceeded to graciously indulge me in the details as I nervously took stock of the long line of folks still waiting their turn for a photo. Of course, he signed the bill.

That rider directed the Forest Service to sell a quantity of timber sales, some in ancient forest and others in areas burned by wildfires, regardless of other laws. This was a low point in the movement, and it led to another wave of protests in 1996.

CNW organized some of these protests. I attended one, my first in eight years, with my infant daughter, Jessie, on a rainy day in the Olympic Mountains. I did not get arrested but instead was there to support the intentional and dignified arrest action of several state agency employees. My view by this time was that civil disobedience would be most impactful if carried out not by angry rebels, but by diverse and respected community leaders. I argued this in a speech I delivered at a forest conference in southern Oregon. I titled it, "Civil Disobedience as Tactic, Not Culture." My point was that our goals and message have broad appeal, and that our movement needed and could attain corresponding broad support. The deliberately countercultural appearance and behavior of frontline forest activists was unhelpful. A group of social scientists has recently documented this effect in an article called, "The Activist's Dilemma: Extreme Protest Actions Reduce Popular Support for Social Movements."

I regard the gold standard in effective civil disobedience to be the civil rights movement under Dr. Martin Luther King, Jr. and his Southern Christian Leadership Conference. Their signature protests included marches to polling places and sit-ins at lunch counters, staged and framed to convey common values like voting and dining. Those protesters wore jackets and ties. They upheld decorum to draw empathy rather than contrast from the American public. In his "Letter from Birmingham Jail," King notably includes negotiation and "self-purification" in the steps to precede direct action. Civil disobedience in the tradition of Gandhi and King involves breaking laws that are unjust and accepting the legal consequences to draw public sympathy and political support.

Sadly, despite my modest urgings, the forest protest movement evolved to more radical tactics. I have little inside perspective, but the timing shows a circumstantial relationship between 1996 protests of timber projects sold under the logging rider outside Eugene, Oregon and violent property crimes, including fire-bombings, starting shortly after that were committed in the name of Earth Liberation Front. When the World Trade Organization met in Seattle in 1999, havoc was wreaked by black-clad anarchists reputed to have been based in Eugene, undermining the nonviolent plans of leaders in a coalition that involved organized labor and others. These "black bloc" elements have continued to appear, including in the 2020 Black Lives Matter protests that followed the killing of George Floyd. I shudder to think of what Gandhi or King would have felt to see protests in their tradition of discipline and moral nonviolence corrupted and undermined by people in masks breaking store windows and carrying on in ways that we might expect to see from agents provocateur with the malevolent intent of defaming a movement on behalf of entrenched power and interests. Similarly, the young climate activists who have, for instance, glued themselves to famous works of art, should bill for their services the fossil fuel companies that stand to benefit from the PR fallout of such foolishly offensive tactics. When your tactics resemble those which adversaries would surreptitiously use to tarnish your movement, it is time to back off.

Back to my personal story. I learned a lot from my activist years. I learned how to organize and lead, ways to withstand inevitable disappointments, how to raise funds and minds, how to attract media coverage, and more. Those were all results of my empowerment. Perhaps more importantly, I also learned optimism. Had we not succeeded wildly in protecting ancient forests, I might not have the sustaining hope that I retain even today. I restate that I am not proud of everything I did in my twenties. Some actions that I was part of were callous. I regret that. But I learned from those too.

5

Saving the Forest Through the Trees

The wildlands of the Loomis State Forest
(photo courtesy of Conservation Northwest)

"The Forest Service manages our public lands like a good old boys' club. A checkbook won't get you in; you need a chainsaw." That's what I said, sporting a lumberjack's red flannel shirt, on *NBC News* with Tom Brokaw.

It was summer of 1996, and my organization had submitted the highest bid for a timber sale on the Okanogan National Forest. Our plan was to pay for the contract and *not* cut down the trees. Nobody had done that before, but as a proud new father, I was full of zeal. It was a fun story that the press couldn't resist. I saw it as a lark that exposed flawed economics that were harming our forests and streams.

The Thunder Mountain Timber Sale was to cut down trees that had burned in a 1995 wildfire. These trees were in roadless, high-elevation lynx habitat, the same area that prompted our 1988 protest (riot dogs and cow dung in the AC). The trees were also of low monetary value due to a weak national economy. My staff ecologist explained to me that because the project was covered by the aforementioned clearcut rider (which undercut environmental laws during this period), there was nothing further we could do.

"The shame of it is," Evan Frost temple numbersaid, "they're not likely to get any bids even at fire-sale pricing."

I responded with a laugh. "Somebody will bid. Us!"

Gingrich's Republican Party had taken a dark turn away from conservation values that had previously been a third rail of American politics, challenging my optimism that science would increasingly inform policy. Needing a new trick that might appeal to Republicans in power, we turned to economics.

I had read about how federal projects that were harmful to nature sometimes cost the public more than they returned. Taxpayers covered not only the costs of Forest Service staff to plan and administer projects, but also construction of roads into steep, wild country where, like on Thunder Mountain, the value of the logs fell far short of recouping the outlay. Most Republican leaders didn't care, but some in the truly libertarian wing of the party did. If we told the right story, could we split them off?

Paul Allen, co-founder of Microsoft, had recently launched his Paul G. Allen Forest Protection Foundation. I sent a letter proposing that the foundation bankroll such tactics with an escrow account on which CNW or other groups could draw if we won non-logging rights to federal timber sales. I included in the letter a reference to similar state lands adjacent to Thunder Mountain which the managing agency, Washington's Department of Natural Resources (DNR), was under pressure to log, suggesting that maybe something could be done there too. That letter earned me a meeting with the foundation's staff, Bill Pope, who had been an early attorney at Microsoft. Bill was excited about the state lands part of the proposal but was unable to get traction with his boss, so nothing initially came of this contact.

Elsewhere, my antics helped us make some headway. I became popular in the office of John Kasich (R, OH), at that point the idealistic young chair of the House Budget Committee. I was invited to visit him at his desk one day.

"What do environmentalists think of me?" he asked.

"We see you as an ally. Perverse subsidies harm both taxpayers and nature." I thought that was the right thing to say but instead had inadvertently offended him.

"It's not just about that," Kasich said. "It's about the beauty of nature."

He went on to tell a story of a nature experience that had moved him. It touched me that he cared. Another ally for nature!

The Forest Service ultimately sold Thunder Mountain to a logging outfit, ending with the usual stumps. Efforts like mine to focus attention on the budget impacts of below-cost timber sales did eventually get results. The best outcome was in 2001, when after groundwork had been laid by Congressman Norm Dicks, Clinton adopted a new policy that protected roadless areas on national forests nationwide, thus curtailing much of the roadbuilding that comprises the biggest ecological impact and taxpayer subsidy to logging. But Thunder Mountain led to something else too.

Things were getting interesting in the Loomis State Forest, the land I described as adjacent to Thunder Mountain in my letter to Paul Allen's foundation. State public lands are managed to generate revenue for specific trusts, including construction of public schools. The state was under legal and political pressure to log in the remaining wild areas of the Loomis Forest, which would require building about one hundred miles of logging roads into wild country. In 1997, we sued to block that plan. The elected head of the Department of Natural Resources was a progressive Democrat, Jennifer Belcher. She had followed, and was intrigued by, our Thunder Mountain effort and called me one evening to explore options. The result was a settlement agreement allowing us to protect twenty-five thousand acres from roads and logging if we could pay the trusts the fair market value of the trees within fifteen months, including a payment of over one hundred thousand dollars in earnest money due within three months.

I had no way to know it at the time, but this would entail raising over eighteen million dollars. At that point, in 1998, our annual budget was about one percent of that, and my board of directors had no reason to expect we could pull this off. But my second daughter was about to be born, and I was again full of zeal. I made a couple calls, including one to Bill Pope. I asked if he thought we could succeed. Bill's forceful optimism had no underlying rational basis. Still, I signed the settlement decree and went to work.

We put together a great team. We branded the Loomis Forest "Washington's Little Yellowstone" for its value to carnivores like lynx. Our office manager, Mary Humphries, proposed and then implemented an innovative grassroots fundraising plan focused around house parties. The success of that strategy launched Mary into a career as a fundraising professional.

To reach our lofty challenge, we needed not just grassroots support, but big gifts. We had the luck to be campaigning during the height of the first tech bubble. A generation of Microsoft executives and engineers had just reached a point in their careers when they had both the means and public spirit to begin engaging in philanthropy. Bill Pope introduced us to some of those people by hosting a dinner in a Seattle restaurant. I also reached out to the only other person I knew at Microsoft, a mid-level engineer who was involved in conservation. Jeff threw himself into the effort, organizing a campaign of elaborate matching gifts within the corporation that landed donations from hundreds of its employees. We relied on a saintly emissary from the Loomis Forest, Mark Skatrud, to help carry our message. Mark, a calm man with long blond hair, seems somehow elfish even at his average height and build. He lived in a cabin bordering the Loomis Forest, and when not working as a carpenter, his hobby was tracking wildlife like lynx. His firsthand testimony grounded our pitch, making it more believable, urgent, and human.

For an exciting year, we were the darling underdog cause.

Media were interested in new tech philanthropy, so our seven-figure gifts were covered on the front page of *The Seattle Times* and sometimes in national press, compounding momentum. This buzz also energized grassroots giving, which in turn impressed and encouraged big donors. More than thirty-five hundred people contributed, most of them in amounts of a few hundred dollars.

Many people asked whether it was fair that private funds were needed to ransom habitat on public lands. Indeed, the policy underlaying this requirement rested on a dubious interpretation of the Washington State Constitution. It required the state, as trustee, to have undivided loyalty to the specific fiduciary trusts that gained revenue from the logging of public land. My answer to the question was that we had to protect the Loomis wildlands now and then fix the corrupt law later. It took twenty-three years, but with tireless and tenacious focus from Peter Goldman and other attorneys, CNW eventually won a landmark 2022 ruling from the Supreme Court of Washington. The ruling holds that the state has discretion to balance fiduciary trusts with larger public interests. If the Loomis showdown were to happen today, the state would have the discretion to protect the habitat without requiring that the fiduciary trusts be compensated. But back to our story.

In mid-1999, we were still a million bucks short of the required $13.1 million as the deadline approached. One donor, a tech executive named Bruce who I had met at the dinner Bill Pope hosted, had already given over two million dollars. He let me know in his blasé, off-handed way that he was willing to do more. I replied that he shouldn't have to, as Paul Allen—who had been aware of the issue since even before the campaign launched—had yet to give. I was standing by the payphone in the foyer of the state's Natural Resources Building as the minutes ticked down. Soon I would have to report our status to the Board of Natural Resources. When no savior rang, I dialed Bruce. He agreed to the last million. I then strutted down the hall to the hearing room and told the board that we had the money and were ready to complete the deal.

They replied that due to an appraisal dispute, they had decided to raise the price by $3.5 million. After fifteen months of hard work and the elation of having reached our original goal in a photo finish, my heart sank at the dispiriting news. Outrage and headlines ensued.

The next day, I got a call from Sue Coliton, who had taken Bill Pope's spot as head of Paul Allen's foundation. She asked about our plans.

"I don't know," I said. "Yesterday, I could have told you that this was a good deal. I'm not sure that's still true. We're looking at legal options."

Sue encouraged me to hold off on any decision and said she would call again the next afternoon.

The following day, I had lunch with Fred Munson, who ran the Loomis Forest Fund for me. Fred is a masterful campaign leader with roots at Greenpeace. Cheerful and idealistic but tough and thorough on business, Fred was invaluable on three CNW campaigns in the years around the turn of the millennium. During a lunch discussion, we speculated on how much Paul Allen might give. This was a Lucy-and-the-football conversation, as we had been expecting a gift from Allen since my call with Bill Pope fifteen months earlier. We dared to let ourselves dream of a million bucks.

We had shuffled back to the office by the time Sue called, and I put her on the speakerphone.

"Mr. Allen will provide the full three-point-five million dollars," Sue announced.

Fred and I looked at one another slack-jawed.

"Are you there?" Sue asked.

The Loomis Forest campaign was transformative. It told a story of how in the modern economy, vertical trees could be worth more than horizontal ones. It also earned me a reputation as a bit of a miracle worker, at least among people not aware that the accounting for those eighteen million dollars (including campaign expenses) was done by our young office manager, Debbie (B.S. in biology), in a handwritten ledger. I got a call from my friend Pat McMahon, a reporter who had covered the campaign for *USA Today*, to ask what new horizons I would be off to. He expected me to jump to a bigger ship. I told him that I was right where I wanted to be and had no plans to move anywhere. My ambition remained to pursue the mission of CNW, to keep the Northwest wild, and there was no better seat from which to do that than the one I already occupied.

Within a year, Fred and I launched a new and even more ambitious campaign: to fix a land ownership problem created by Abraham Lincoln that threatened to cut asunder the ecosystem of Washington's Cascade Mountains. The government had subsidized a railroad to the West Coast by granting land to the Northern Pacific Railroad in a checkerboard pattern of alternating square miles. These sections of land were now, over a century later, being clearcut to create square-mile gaps in the forest. Our goal was to buy key parcels along paths of known wildlife movement, thereby stitching together connections between the forested mountains to the north and south.

I credit Charlie Raines with seeding the idea for this campaign. It happened during the gala celebration of our Loomis victory, which we held at the Seattle Aquarium. The appetizers and speeches were finished, and I was with my two toddler daughters in front of the octopus tank when Charlie, a Sierra

Club leader and consummate schmoozer and nudger, sidled over to see what I had in mind for tackling next. The "next" thing was far from my mind on this celebratory evening. But when Charlie suggested fixing the Cascades checkerboard problem, I immediately agreed.

Between 2000 and 2005, this campaign—a large coalition we led called the Cascades Conservation Partnership—raised over eighteen million dollars in private gifts, repeating our Loomis number. We took the big step of adding an actual bookkeeper to the staff. Paul Allen and Bruce each gave another three and half million dollars to start us off strong. Through a fortunate staff connection and a lot of hard work, we hosted the Seattle premier of *The Two Towers*, the second film in *The Lord of the Rings* series, in Paul Allen's iconic downtown theater, Cinerama. I finally got to meet Paul that night and was in the process of thanking him for his generous gifts when Bill Gates interrupted us. (I had already met Bill and Melinda at the concession stand, thanking them for their $100,000 Loomis gift.) Gates and Allen were then chatting until they were interrupted by Peter Gabriel, the rock star. Before the film, the audience sat through speeches from the CEO of New Line Cinema, the stars who played Gimli the Dwarf and Sam the Hobbit, and me.

We were making great initial progress until the tech bubble burst early in 2000. We carried on. For this campaign, we wanted private funds to be matched by public ones. So, in addition to courting big donations, we ran a grassroots campaign that generated thousands of small gifts and letters to Congress. We had an incredible public outreach team, including a young UW graduate student with boundless energy named Jen Watkins, that had a presence in countless public parades, fairs, and other events to keep up the grassroots pressure on Congress. We also hired high-end government affairs advisors (e.g. lobbyists) specializing in each side of the political aisle in Washington, D.C., and I made many trips east for lobbying meetings. My kids were young, so I couldn't stand to be away long. I took red-eye, coast-to-coast flights that landed in D.C. just before morning meetings, then flew home that same night or the next day. It all worked, winning earmarked appropriations to the Forest Service that totaled over $65 million during the campaign, resulting in over forty-five thousand acres of connecting forest habitat, shifting from corporate ownership to public national forest. This solved the rift that had been threatening to bisect the Cascades ecosystem.

Key to our success was that Washington's two senators each had powerful seats. The Republicans held the Senate during the first couple years, and Washington's Slade Gorton chaired the key House Appropriations Subcommittee on Interior, Environment and Related Agencies. Slade was no liberal, but our campaign had some Republican donors and cachet. Slade was also in a tough race for reelection against Democrat Maria Cantwell, and he needed some green cred.

One October day in 2002, I was sitting in my Bellingham office when a call came from Senator Gorton's chief of staff. "Mitch, Slade wants to give you guys another seventeen million dollars, but you're going to have to thank him publicly."

Ouch.

I'm a liberal Democrat and had donated to Cantwell. I had even arranged for Carole King to perform at a private fundraiser for her. The last thing I wanted was to help Slade Gorton peel off enough votes to win. But with my loyalty to the Cascades, I consented. The Forest Service was given an additional seventeen million dollars with which to buy key acres in the habitat corridor. We held a press conference in which Charlie Raines and I thanked Senator Gorton, even as the Sierra Club protested outside. Cantwell ended up winning that election by about two thousand votes, saving Charlie and me from purgatory. From that point on, Senator Patty Murray (D, WA) took over as champion to fund land purchases reconnecting the Cascades.

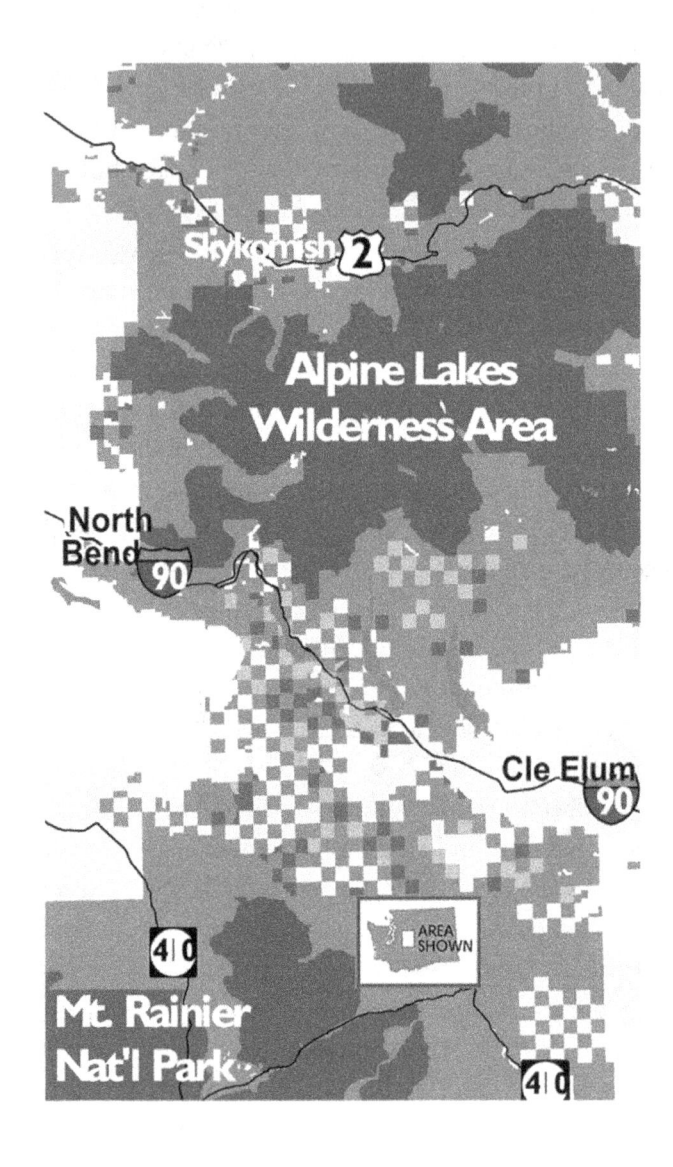

There were a couple of great unforeseen benefits to our successful Cascades Partnership effort. First, it catalyzed a body of work that resulted in at least one (a second is pending) signature wildlife overpass and multiple huge underpasses on Interstate 90 east of Snoqualmie Pass. These structures complement the habitat protections to comprise the wildlife corridors that connect the North and South Cascades which lie respectively on either side of the interstate.

One version of that story is the nexus of two incredible extroverts, CNW's Jen Watkins (introduced above) and a Forest Service wildlife biologist named Patty Garvey-Darda. Either of them alone can take over a meeting with a firehose of ideas conveyed with infectious enthusiasm, selfless commitment, and guaranteed follow-through. Together, they whip up a funnel cloud. In a happy coincidence, while we were working to protect connecting habitat on either side of the interstate, the Washington State Department of Transportation was starting plans to widen and straighten the highway itself for traffic efficiency and safety. Patty knew that WSDOT would require cooperation from the Forest Service for staging areas and other uses of national forest land. That gave her leverage to push for wildlife mitigations like highway crossings.

As the work of the Cascades Partnership wound down and that team broke up, we knew we wanted to keep Jen. We also kept Charlie Raines under contract and tasked the two of them with leading a new I-90 Wildlife Bridges Coalition. We found support among commercial interests who understood the value of their truck drivers not having to worry about animals on the highway, and we found bipartisan leaders in the legislature who also saw the upsides. It helped that a couple of WSDOT leaders were forward thinking. Brian White, the regional director, became an advocate within WSDOT for wildlife crossings and a partner for us in addressing obstacles. Meanwhile, the head of the agency, Secretary of Transportation Doug MacDonald, was a visionary who was delighted to advance the wildlife agenda. He even signed a Secretarial Order directing that wildlife passage be an objective of all major transportation projects in the state.

In the end, WSDOT not only built the structures but viewed them with pride. Wildlife conservation is a public value that road engineers can come to embrace along with safety, efficiency, and durability. This stretch of highway came to be seen as the continent's leading model for wildlife mitigation, providing not only for the passage of large mammals and of fish, but even small mammals and amphibians. In the ensuing years, WSDOT personnel took the message on the road, evangelizing the value of wildlife crossings at conferences of road engineers. We continue today to build on this foundation of success, with projects and plans to mitigate highways around the state, including crossings on Interstate 5 in two places between Olympia and Portland. These crossings will someday provide connectivity between the Cascades and the Chehalis River Valley and ultimately the Olympic Peninsula. Had we not undertaken the Cascades Partnership, this chain of successes likely would never have come into being.

Recently, I picked up a book from 1996 that had long been on my shelves—*Impressions of the North Cascades: Essays about a Northwest Landscape,* edited by John C. Miles. One of its final essays was written by me. I was going off on the vision thing, about the need for, and challenges of, protecting connected ecosystems. I wrote, "Linkages between large ecosystems are a daunting prospect. . . . To link the North Cascades to the . . . Central Cascades involves spanning Interstate 90 and making sense out of the checkerboard of private/public ownerships, a legacy of century-old land grants to rail barons. **Planning for establishment of these corridors must begin now, even if such plans cannot realistically be carried out for decades or possibly centuries.**" Well, we got that one done decades or possibly centuries ahead of my forecasted schedule. So, why would I ever cast doubt again?

I said the Cascades Partnership had two unforeseen benefits. The second was that it firmed up our relationships with dozens of generous and public-spirited people from Microsoft and elsewhere who appreciated our culture of boldness and pragmatism, evidenced by objective measures of success on the ground. For two decades since, we have maintained relationships with lots of these folks, many becoming personal friends. Paul Bannick, a renowned wildlife photographer and himself a former tech worker, has been effective as our director of major gifts throughout this period. This core support gave us the means to not be dependent on inflammatory fundraising tactics common to many nonprofit and political groups. Not having to sell outrage to our base gave us flexibility to explore tactics solely for their effectiveness. Through this, we developed a new brand of conservation that I had not foreseen.

Part II

Collaboration

6

Collaboration: Its Origin Story

Field tour on Gifford Pinchot National Forest
(photo courtesy of Conservation Northwest)

Quick recap: In 1998, CNW was a small, garden variety, regional conservation group with an annual budget of about a quarter million bucks. By 2005, we had raised over thirty-six million dollars from private donors, leveraging an additional sixty-five million dollars in congressional appropriations, with the net effects of saving twenty-five thousand acres of Loomis Forest wildlands and transferring over forty-five thousand central Cascades acres into national forest to be managed as connectivity habitat. You would be rational to expect that this Herculean effort consumed all our focus. You would also be wrong. CNW has always run a half-dozen or more programs, and some of this work would have a transformative impact.

Since 1994, Dave Werntz, our director of science and conservation, has led a team that has watchdogged Forest Service timber projects in Washington. I hired Dave at first to make the most of the Northwest Forest Plan by emphasizing its most promising language and allying with forward-thinking agency staff within key Forest Service offices. This is significant, as many of our West Coast peers focused on the plan's failure to outright protect all old-growth forest, in essence resisting the plan, while we elevated it.

The complex stew that comprises Dave can be boiled down to two primary ingredients: Minnesotan with an analytic personality. Put an encyclopedic mind into the generously progressive spirit of a Minnesota social democrat, and you've got Dave. If your throat is sore, Dave is eager to share the what and why of the latest remedies, Mr. Spock-like. What's the weather doing? Dave memorized and can interpret the week's satellite data. Dave's need for logic and a just world extends to all things. He is constantly parsing events verbally, seeking sense and order within the chaos. That's a bit hard for me, as while Dave is jabbering, verbally processing what just happened, I am often trying to shift the focus to what's going to happen next. Maybe I get a bit impatient at times. But for three decades, we have made it work.

We met in the 1980s. While I was leading protests, Dave was a graduate student mapping old-growth and spotted owl habitat. When I needed somebody to get the most out of the Northwest Forest Plan, Dave's familiarity with relevant science and his attention to detail made him a natural fit. The plan has its most sweeping protections on the two national forests of Northwest Washington because they sit at the northern end of the owl's range, where it is most imperiled. However, on the Gifford Pinchot National Forest, in Washington's southern Cascades, much ancient forest remained outside of the plan's protected reserves. And those big trees were still being cut down.

Named for the progressive associate of President Theodore Roosevelt who is most responsible for the origins of the national forest system and its first leader, the Gifford Pinchot National Forest was a timber breadbasket. Lacking the geologic grandeur of the North Cascades and Olympics and tucked between the nature playgrounds preferred by Seattle or Portland, the GPNF was low on the conservation radar. Even today, it has much less protected wilderness or hiker traffic than those other forests. But in the campaign to implement the Northwest Forest Plan, it became a focus of a new generation of activists. They protested with tree-sits and road blockades, and we helped a bit. But the new generation was also intent on working in the communities, reaching out to labor and community leaders, and advancing social justice.

One group doing that work had a small staff that included Jasmine Minbashian and others, and a volunteer named Jen Watkins, who you already met. CNW merged with that group in 2000, with those folks becoming staff of CNW. Jasmine grew up in Seattle, the granddaughter of one of the Shah of Iran's top generals. She earned her master's degree at England's venerable Cambridge University after her undergrad at Bellingham's Western Washington University, where she was on the tennis team. She kicked my butt in tennis every time we played except once, when I stole a match in gusty winds that confounded her.

The job of Dave's team was originally to use carrots and sticks to get the most out of the Northwest Forest Plan. Admittedly, we used mostly sticks in the early days, filing administrative appeals and lawsuits to slow, modify, or block the timber projects that were most egregious in harming ancient forest. The new cohort wanted to dangle more carrots. While they were just a decade or so younger than Dave and me, they came of age under different influences and saw with fresher eyes.

The team attended a field trip to the Gifford Pinchot National Forest with executives from local timber companies that were buying federal trees for their sawmills. They returned with big news: The reviled timber beasts no longer wanted big logs! They said that smaller trees, regrown into land clearcut decades earlier, now met their manufacturing needs. This presented the opportunity to work with timber leaders to reform entrenched pockets of old guard within the Forest Service.

Being somewhat entrenched myself, I was at first skeptical. But my resistance wore down, and I let them explore the opportunity. The youth turned out to be right, with the result being a new era of collaboration on national forests. I remained a bit cynical even as the results impressed me, referring to collaboration as passive-aggressive conservation. While we had formerly barked, "Leave the old-growth alone, you sons of bitches," now we entreated, "Let's work together to restore to second-growth, you beautiful people." In retrospect, I kick myself for not seeing this as a perfect expression of an indirect strategic approach. This is what my strategy studies had advised me to pursue! And in due time we fully embraced it.

Maybe this is the right time to mention the one notable lesson I try to teach and follow in my work. I call it Righeimer's Rule, as I got it from my freshman year football coach, Ralph Righeimer. He was chewing out an offensive lineman for lazy play and shouted, "If you miss your block, you can still hit somebody! And do it at full speed!" Those words stuck with me in a way much larger than Coach intended: If you fully commit to your decisions, even bad ones can produce good outcomes. I guess that makes me pragmatic and adaptive rather than doctrinaire.

The Gifford Pinchot National Forest is where we worked to bring the idea of collaboration to life. With partners, we founded the Gifford Pinchot Working Group, which I believe was the first local national forest management collaboration. CNW was represented on its board, which included other conservationists, a labor leader, and notably John Squires, a resident of a local timber town. John cared about the forest but cared more about his town. He helped us understand the changes occurring to schools, services, and the very livability of timber towns that were declining due not only to conservation policies but also automation and economic forces that drive centralization of mill infrastructure. The point of a collaboration is to genuinely listen enough to diverse perspectives to understand their interests, find the common ground among them, and pursue policies—such as logging of second-growth trees and local manufacturing—

that advance that common ground. Interests is the key word, contrasted with "positions." The latter can be inflexible, while the former can possibly be met through creative accommodation. Interests can foster collaboration, while positions can engender gridlock.

It was fascinating to learn how much we had in common with timber industry and community interests, including frustration with a Forest Service that had become adrift. It was clear to anyone paying attention that the sweet spot in public benefit was to be had by the agency selling rights to log stands of trees under a century in age, but good leadership is required to achieve even common-sense outcomes. I remember a contemporaneous newspaper article about the new collaboration on the Gifford Pinchot National Forest. An old-guard agency forester had the temerity to be quoted on the record with his real opinion. "But if we do that (cut mature but not old trees), the environmentalists will have won!" We had to work through such obstacles by empowering more thoughtful agency staff.

Meanwhile, a few of us were led by Andy Kerr to collaborate at a giant scale to reach a regional grand bargain with leaders in Oregon's timber industry. Andy entered the movement a decade before me by co-founding a leading Oregon conservation group, and he was central to the ancient forest battle. When *TIME* magazine covered the issue, they included a sidebar on the ever-provocative Andy. The article pointed out that some in the timber industry mocked him for resembling a spotted owl, to which Andy replied, "That really ruffles my feathers." He had been a voice in my ear for some time, including the initial suggestion that we resolve the threat to the Loomis Forest via purchasing the rights.

Our idea was to protect all ancient forests while having logging focused on second-growth. Our hope was that if we struck a deal, Senator Ron Wyden (D, OR) would shepherd it through Congress. The secret negotiations seemed promising enough that we contracted an expert to model how much timber could be produced by cutting only second-growth trees under the strongest safeguards for streams and habitat features. His report showed that practicing only the best forestry in only the least-sensitive forests would still produce plenty of logs. The activist community did not embrace the report as warmly as we hoped, with some objecting to logging even second-growth. The debate foreshadowed a rift that endured in various forms. In the end, we fell short of agreement with the timber executives, so the grand bargain was never launched. The Northwest Forest Plan remains today an administrative policy not enshrined in statute. The permanent disposition of ancient forests remains in play even now. President Biden advanced a Presidential Executive Order to inventory and protect old forests on federal lands across America, but the result did not get fully baked before Trump retook office, ultimately providing little change.

This is a good spot to explain that CNW operated without a strategic plan for our first fifteen years. I doubt I had even been familiar with the concept. We had a mission (protect and connect wildlands from the Washington Coast to the Canadian Rockies and restore the region's iconic wildlife) and focus, and somehow seemed to be having impact, at least on the western half of our turf. But it was time to come up with an approach that could improve conservation progress in the drier eastern half of the region. In 2002, the CNW board and staff held a retreat to develop our first strategic plan. The result was a strategic restructuring. In 2003, we merged with yet another smaller organization, this time in northeast Washington, taking on its staff and a key role in the collaborative Northeast Washington Forest Coalition (more on that later). We changed our name to Conservation Northwest, hoping to soften our brand for broader appeal. And we adopted new public messaging with the same intent.

I brought the approach into my personal life, taking up deer hunting in part so I could better understand and communicate with the diverse interests in the big tent. There was another thought with all this change. It came from my friend Tom Campion, a longtime member of CNW's board of directors and a generous conservation donor from wealth he derived as leader of Zumiez, Inc. After returning from a conservation gala in Montana, Tom described how the room included hunters, anglers, and even ranchers. That struck me hard, resonating with memories from my time in Bozeman, when Montana was rugged yet progressive. And it contrasted sharply with the conservation politics of Washington, where the diversity of wildlands advocates ranged only from hiker to birder, while sportsmen were regarded as rednecks and ranchers as welfare gentry. I wanted Washington's conservation movement to be a bigger tent that better reflected the political breadth of people who value wild nature, even if not for the same reasons or in the same ways.

Broad coalitions are another form of indirect strategy, as they require the finding of common ground on which to build the big tent, rather than the attempt to impose policies through identity politics and sanctimonious moralizing, trademarks of the counterproductive liberal posture. Collaboration and coalitions do not describe all the work that CNW does, nor all our successes. We use a range of tactics from litigation to grassroots organizing to legislative lobbying to property acquisition to collaboration, with a pretty good overall batting average. In upcoming chapters, I will parse what my experience has taught me about situational conservation strategy.

While all this collaboration was occurring, love was in the air. Dave married Jasmine, and you will see their names in the pages ahead. Regan Smith and Pete Nelson, who were key players in these events, also got married and have gone on to amazing careers in conservation. In fact, the cohort of CNW staff and partners described in this chapter has had tremendous continuing impact. Demis Foster, Heidi Eisenhour, Jen Watkins, and James Johnston remain leaders in conservation and related endeavors. So are many other former interns and staff of CNW. This gives me a feeling of great satisfaction. Over all these years of so many successes and frustrations, we never once missed payroll and were able to provide for many good people to own homes, raise families, and fulfill aspirations to have a meaningful life of helping protect and restore wild nature.

7

Finding Common Ground in the Woods

Prescribed burn in Naches area, 2016
(photo by Jason Emhoff, USFS)

Maurice Williamson was a crusty old codger, and he wouldn't have minded me saying so. He passed away in March of 2024 in Colville, Washington, where he had raised his family during a career as a consulting forester. Colville is the largest small city in northeastern Washington, ninety minutes northwest of Spokane. That part of the state aligns more with the conservative politics of Idaho than with western Washington, and Maurice was proud to fit in. He knew and cursed my name in the 1980s. When I was organizing protests and dishing out provocative and polarizing soundbites, Maurice was advising private parties—from families with a few acres to corporate timber barons—on logging practices. He wasn't on my radar until 2004.

Our worlds converged in the Northeast Washington Forest Coalition, or NEWFC. When CNW began working in the area, this collaborative had just been established to explore and actualize new common ground between timber and conservation interests on the Colville National Forest, which spans much of northeast Washington. This common ground was unique in occurring at the scales of both the forest stand and the larger landscape. Northeast Washington is a mix of dry lowlands with ponderosa pine forests that require frequent fire to remove competing undergrowth, and higher elevations with wetter mixed-conifer forests. There was broad agreement by this time that dry forests of northeast Washington, like those across the interior West, needed careful active management. Such management often includes removing small trees and using fire to clean up the brush, seedlings, and twigs, restoring a structure of fewer large pine trees with lots of space and not much fuel underneath. Dry forests have suffered badly from a century of mismanagement in which managers cut down the big trees and left behind small ones while also suppressing wildfire. The resulting crowded stands of smaller trees are subject to water stress, disease, and uncharacteristically hot and large fires, especially in today's warmer climate. These are among the reasons why Indians set fire to these forests for the past ten thousand years, as I will discuss in detail later.

Fortunately, today we have technology to produce wood products from small trees, allowing logging to focus on removing those but leaving the bigger ones. Over time, with help from low-intensity fire (natural or managed) every few years, this can restore dry forests toward pre-colonial conditions of ecological health. It's harder than it may seem, as roads built for logging access can impact wildlife and especially the condition of streams and fish. Logging that is too aggressive or not followed with controlled fire can perpetuate the fuel problems that elevate wildfire risk. Some of Washington's worst recent wildfires burned heavily through private and tribal industrial timberland, which is consistent with findings from research. Sage-steppe grassland ecosystems are also burning heavily of late, highlighting the warmer and drier climate. Careful logging and cattle grazing (if focused on seasonal consumption of invasive cheatgrass) can improve the situation, while poor practices worsen it. Lastly, homes now pockmark the woods, constraining the use of fire as a management tool. We will never be able to resume the carefree Indian practice of letting fires rip, though we should get as close to that as is practical.

At the landscape level, higher elevations in the mountain ranges of northeast Washington are largely roadless and therefore protected from roadbuilding and most logging under the

Roadless Area Protection Policy adopted by President Clinton at the end of his second term. But unlike western Washington, with its three large national parks and millions of acres of designated wilderness, eastern Washington has very little permanently protected land. The founders of NEWFC all agreed with a general principle offered by Duane Vaagen, the second-generation leader of a family-owned Colville-based timber company: Roughly a third of the Colville National Forest should be managed in each of these conditions: (1) protected as wild, (2) actively restored to healthy forests to be maintained by fire rather than logging, and (3) actively and indefinitely managed for timber production using excellent forestry. NEWFC continues to collaboratively pursue a version of this formula today, with CNW staff still fully engaged.

Back to Maurice, who engaged deeply in NEWFC for the many years that his health and vitality allowed. He was at first openly disdainful and skeptical of my staff and our agenda. He had his perceptions about me and perhaps conservationists in general, informed by painful experiences of the `80s and `90s. The direction I give staff in these collaborations is to engage honorably. We rely on applying the best available science to negotiate and implement the best practices. In instances where science is unclear, we are transparent about that and try to learn together by both engaging experts and trying small-scale field experiments. Our strictest rule is to *never move the goalposts*. We are to negotiate aggressively using our best arguments and tactics, but then stand by whatever agreement is struck. Behaving honorably builds trust and reciprocation.

Special interests often shift their goalposts. Once one concession is won, they demand a new one. Politicians do it, as do business interests. None pains me more than watching peer conservation groups do so. Groups will sue to block a shift in legal status for a rebounded species, to apply a new rule to an old plan, or to force another question to be answered within the tome of an environmental study. Biological arguments can always be found, often with much legitimacy. But there is a cost. Our leverage stems from the support of the public and respect of partners. If we don't stand by our agreements, why would anyone spend effort to dialogue with and accommodate us?

Maurice had to see it to believe it. Like my staff, Maurice negotiated hard, representing his views and knowledge from a life dedicated to his profession. It did not surprise him that we would, for instance, push for protection of big trees and streamside buffers, citing scientific research. He would gruffly push back, citing contrary research and experience. That is how the work is done, by arguing, listening, and reaching accommodation. The poison was that Maurice assumed we would look for ways to later exit or modify those accommodations when it suited us. When he instead observed my staff, most notably the diligent and earnest David Heflick, sadly now deceased, honorably standing by agreements, his posture changed.

There was a particular day when Maurice smiled and pulled out a bottle of whiskey, probably Old Crow, his favorite brand. We had won his respect. Over time, he became a friend, each of us enduring playful insults from the other.

The NEWFC collaboration fostered a period of great productivity on the Colville National Forest. The forest had excellent leadership who appreciated the cues the collaborative sent regarding what projects were of greatest benefit and least concern, and also which did not measure up and needed specific work. Working together to produce only projects featuring excellent forestry for restorative objectives, the forest moved from a national laggard to a national leader in timber output. Almost twenty years on now, we have seen good days and bad, opportunities and challenges. The secret sauce of collaboration is quality relationships built on trust. Not just among the collaborative group, but also with public agency leaders. The Forest Service has a policy of shifting its leaders around the country, which imposes turnover and disruption in those relationships. There are also internal incentives within the agency that create headwinds, such as performance reviews that reward personnel for hitting timber targets instead of ecological ones. On whole, it requires hard work, patience, and persistence. Its greatest allure is that it stands in contrast to the polarizing alternative.

Like my relationship to collaboration as a tactic, my one with Maurice was a long journey. Looking back, I would not change a thing about it. While we succeeded in finding common ground and getting a lot done together, we didn't change Maurice's core values, and he didn't change mine. The last time I saw him, he was watching a rant on a conservative news channel. He called it "the truth." Still, the benefits of that relationship and others like it include thousands of acres of forests that have been restored toward a more natural and ecologically healthy condition. They also include less political polarization, as we now better understand and appreciate one another and speak up in our communities to counter caricatures now referred to as "othering of out groups." We also learned from one another, and continue to.

Mark Twain said, "It ain't what you don't know that gets you into trouble. It's what you know for sure that just ain't so." We live in a complex world that doesn't always fit into our mental models. The best elixir is a strong dose of other viewpoints, especially those formed through careful study and long experience. I value what I've heard from foresters, ranchers, farmers, hunters, and Indians. I often learn from their viewpoints irrespective of whether I agree with them. It gives me a more complete view of the world and a healthy skepticism of any doctrine, including whatever I'm supposed to believe as an urban liberal environmentalist.

Being educated as a scientist, I believe passionately in the scientific method for its deliberate, controlled search for truth. Modern life would not be possible without what society has learned this way. But the universe hides its truths from even our best queries. For instance, medical science has the benefit that its studies can involve millions of human subjects whose behavior can be somewhat controlled. Yet we now find that even in many of the best epidemiological studies, the results cannot be replicated in subsequent research. The decongestant drug phenylephrine, for example, is now considered ineffective after years of being widely used. If medical science, with all its money and motivation, is still in early days, consider how much more there is to learn about forest ecology and management. We seem to know enough to confidently say, as I did above, that in dry forests we need to protect and reestablish big old trees while reintroducing fire and, where necessary, removing (by chainsaw) small trees to restore more fire-resilient stands. But some forests are drier than others. On north-facing slopes and middle elevations, the forests are of mixed types that confound simple or confident prescriptions. Restoring a whole landscape of drier forest types involves deliberately returning it to a mosaic of forest ages and openings so that the habitat is varied and wildfire is less likely to blow up to megafire proportions. The challenge and complexity of that undertaking is massive. It is hard enough to get predictable returns in a backyard veggie garden, so of course we must be humble about what we think and do over millions of acres of forest knocked off-kilter by fire exclusion and reckless logging. The open and trusting relationships with Maurice and others at the NEWFC table allow for modest trial-and-error learning to advance on this monumental challenge together.

Some of the projects that we at NEWFC have agreed to are opposed and even litigated by other conservation groups. In general, they are more rigid in what they think science indicates, more polar in their views of interests embodied in the collaborative, and less trusting of the Forest Service. Some of their arguments have merit in isolation; others I think are misinformed. But on the whole, I see them as shortsighted, as I will explain in due course.

The success of forest collaboratives like NEWFC in opening dialogue, building trust, and advancing restoration projects caused them to spread rapidly across the western U.S., with mixed results.

As challenging as the landscape ecology of dry forests is, there at least was a body of science in place to build from. There was less clarity on how to move forward on the wetter west side of the region. Our national forests contain hundreds of thousands of acres of forest regrown after clearcut logging up through the 1980s. Research supports thinning these stands to accelerate growth of the remaining trees and expedite stands attaining old-growth characteristics. Research was also clear that we could help fish through measures like removing some roads and stabilizing stream banks. But little attention had been given to how to prioritize work for the greatest return on investment. In 2014, Jen Watkins saw this need and stepped forward.

Jen and Dave Werntz invited leading ecologists and foresters from the U.S. Forest Service, Washington Department of Natural Resources, University of Washington, and elsewhere. This group, which included Jerry Franklin, the luminary forest ecologist who led the design of the Northwest Forest Plan, met until they produced a protocol for restoring westside forest landscapes. The Forest Service has since applied this protocol to a large and exceptional restoration project just northwest of Mount Rainier.

The lessons we are learning from this project can be applied across the wet forests of the Northwest, improving forest habitat and watersheds while providing wood products and jobs for struggling rural communities.

The skills, trust, and reputation gained from our collaborative work on federal lands in southwest and northeast Washington led to another opportunity. In 2006, I got a call from Doug Sutherland, the Republican who was then serving as Washington's Commissioner of Public Lands. He asked if I would serve on a panel of stakeholders to resolve a decade of controversy regarding the forests of Blanchard Mountain. This is a treasured state forest in northwest Washington, where the Cascade Mountains meet the waters of Puget Sound. I signed up.

The forests of Blanchard Mountain are not old-growth, but they are ecologically significant and prized for recreation, being just off Interstate 5 only twenty minutes from Bellingham and an hour from Seattle. The forest had been logged heavily in the early twentieth century, like almost all privately owned forest in the lowlands of western Washington. The land reverted to the county when its owners cut and run, leaving taxes unpaid. The state later agreed to take over reforesting and managing such lands for the benefit of counties. Eight decades on, the now stately forest was wrapped with tranquil trails leading to high points offering stunning views of Puget Sound and the San Juan Islands. Summer weekends find these trails crowded with hikers, equestrians, and mountain bikers. In the late '90s, the Department of Natural Resources kicked a hornet's nest by proposing clearcuts within the heart of Blanchard Mountain. We launched grassroots resistance, with CNW's Lisa McShane catalyzing formation of a local group, Friends of Blanchard Mountain. A political stalemate ensued that lasted several years, leading to that call from Commissioner Sutherland.

The result was the Blanchard Forest Strategies Group. It had a dozen seats filled by leaders from conservation, recreation, timber industry, Skagit County, and the school district that received revenue from the logging of those lands. The sides were clear, with the environmental caucus wanting all old forest protected, and the timber and revenue interests dug in otherwise. We met monthly for well over a year. It was far into that process before we found enough common ground on which to reach agreement. The breakthrough came when we realized that all parties wanted to prevent encroaching residential development from reducing the private timberland that provides logs, jobs, and better habitat for salmon and wildlife than do houses and paved streets.

With that common interest as lubricant, we narrowly reached consensus on a plan to protect from logging about sixteen hundred acres that included most of the older forest on the mountain. We were to jointly request funding from the legislature to compensate the county and school district for the value of the forest, plus additional funds representing the value of the land on which the forest stood. The DNR was to use the latter to purchase private timberland at risk of residential development and manage it perpetually in forestry.

The agreement moved forward with key legislators on board. Some activists felt the agreement should have protected more acreage or even the entirety of state forest around the mountain, most of the remainder of which was plantations of second (or third) growth. They sued to block it. CNW intervened on the side of the state, honoring our commitment. The court eventually ruled against the lawsuit, but the uncertainty it caused limited how much funding the legislature would commit during the interim. Then the economy crashed. It would be almost a decade before the full amount was committed and we could finally celebrate the protected land. During the intervening decade, I organized email campaigns and annual trips to Olympia to lobby for the funds. Those lobby days included the timber leaders and other stakeholders from the Blanchard Forest Strategies Group, all standing by our agreement. All told, the twenty-year effort saved sixteen hundred acres of this scenic, ecological, and recreational gem at a total cost of twelve million dollars.

Might we have done better had we refused to collaborate? Maybe. Maybe not. I am comfortable with, and proud of, the choice I made and its results. But it did get intense. There were heated debates over email listservs on the science and strategic implications thinning westside plantations. This was fine and appropriate. But a line was crossed in 2007, still the early days of collaboration for forest restoration, when a hardline group leveled a harsh accusation at CNW. They compared our work to the Vichy Regime of France, which collaborated with Nazi Germany. If that comparison were to hold, it would mean that CNW was aiding and abetting the forces of destruction of nature, such as companies that profit by harming public forests. I could not help but give this thoughtful consideration, especially since the organization was one that I had previously allied with and even served on the board of. I then replied with a lengthy letter to the leadership of that group, in which I wrote:

> "Can the timber industry be seen as an occupying force on our public land when the Mt. Baker-Snoqualmie National Forest has sustained logging levels less than ten percent of historic highs for about two decades? A better analogy might be to France *after* liberation, when Winston Churchill himself proposed that reconstruction of Europe needed to start with French-German collaboration."

I stand by that comparison. I ended that 2007 letter with the following lines. It troubles me how relevant these words remain almost twenty years on:

> "Our conservation movement faces a curious paradox. Due to climate change, the prospect of utter ecological disaster has never been more urgent, and cause for general despair never more real. Yet we find greater public and political support—at least here in our state—than perhaps ever before. I believe we can make great gains if we, like Churchill did, build our efforts around a spirit that combines realism, shared sacrifice, and hope. We may see protection of what we value if we promote solutions that build support and momentum, rather than ideals that rally a base but ultimately turn away Americans who have grown weary of polarization."

I have come to be a bit humble about what I think we know, even from science. Listening with respect to people who have other views, informed by their experience and observation, is worthwhile. Collaboration fosters that opportunity. If nothing else, we can make one another laugh like Maurice and I did.

8

Wolves Bring Out the Best and Worst in People

Gray wolf
(photo courtesy of Conservation Northwest)

With respect to iconic carnivores, Washington was an underperformer. We had largely lost our gray wolves, wolverines, Pacific fishers, and to some degree grizzly bears and lynx at various points in the twentieth century. That has changed. For me, awareness of the shift came abruptly on a single July day in 2008.

I was hiking with my buddy Tim McHugh on the southwest slopes of Mt. Baker, the volcanic high point of the North Cascades, east of Bellingham. We had come up from the valley of the Middle Fork Nooksack River, following the Ridley Creek Trail as it switchbacked steeply up through forests of lower and mid-elevation, occasionally passing giant sentinel trees, and then into the subalpine. We continued up to alpine, then onto moraine rubble from the glacier, which is of course shrinking.

I had heard about occasional wolverine sightings in the North Cascades. One had even been hit by a car in the 1980s. It seemed likely they were wandering migrants down from Canada, as wolverines can cover incredible distances. Still, the Washington Department of Fish and Wildlife (WDFW) considered them extinct in the state. I never expected to see one myself. I had once come close to an encounter in 1995, on an epic trip in the Northern Rockies of British Columbia, just south of the Yukon border, with a dozen friends, including Tim and my stepsister, Gwen, who visited me many times for such trips from her home on a kibbutz in the south of Israel.

Tim is always the one to see the critters. Same with the trout in deep pools. He has an eye for it. Not that there aren't false alarms. Lots of false alarms. Tim, an excitable boy, will suddenly bark out, "What's that?!" and point to a far slope. My hopes will rise only to be dashed as binoculars reveal the sighting to be maybe a bear-shaped rock. But there is no denying that while I almost always beat Tim in one-on-one hoops, he almost always spots animals, including real ones, before I do.

Our trip in the Northern Rockies was two amazing weeks into deep and wild backcountry, much of it with packhorse and guide support. We tended to travel all in one group, except for one day when we split into two groups, following two different routes to rendezvous later. Tim was in the other group, and damn if they didn't see a wolverine from their trail. I had a deflating feeling of missed opportunity, like being off on the lottery by a single number.

So, here are Tim and me, now slogging through snow on the lower reaches of the Deming Glacier as the midday July sun beat down. Tim suddenly barked out, "What's that?!" Above us on the glacier, maybe one hundred yards distant, something big and round was motoring upslope in second gear. Was it a bear? Was that a hint of white fur? Weird tail. It's a wolverine!

The sighting was short, as she hightailed it away from us. But we climbed up to see and photograph her tracks. Clearly wolverine. My elation was extreme, feeling almost like a rite of passage, this being my first encounter among the class of charismatic megafauna apart from two modest grizzly bear sightings from vehicles.

Back at the car after our hike down, we sped to where I could get a cell signal. My first call was to Scott Fitkin, a WDFW wildlife biologist with extensive carnivore expertise.

"Hey Scott, how are you doing?"

"I'm tired," he said.

"Well, I can perk you up. I just sighted a wolverine on Baker."

"Yeah, well I can top that. I just collared two wolves up the Twisp Valley."

That was an amazingly transformative day. Then, just four months later, I got to be present at the release of the first batch of Pacific fishers into the Elwha Valley of Olympic National Park. This was the leading edge of a successful reintroduction that you will read more about later.

2008 is when Washington became again a legit carnivore state.

My next story comes only a year later, at dusk on a hot day in early July, 2009. We were walking a dusty logging road in the Twisp River Valley in northcentral Washington. I was with my young daughters, Jessie and Carrie, and a visiting nephew, Kevin. We were being led by Scott Fitkin along with biologist Ray Robertson, to see if the Lookout Pack had produced pups that spring.

Wolves had been recolonizing the West for thirty years, twice (including famously in Yellowstone National Park) with human help. CNW had long advocated for wolf recovery in Washington, without success. We celebrated in the summer of 2008 when a motion-activated camera installed by Ray snapped shots of wolf pups in the Twisp area. That was the first documented wolf reproduction in the Pacific Northwest in almost a century. Then Scott trapped and collared the two adult wolves on that momentous July day. DNA tests showed that the parents of the pack had come to this area from the Canadian Rockies and the coast of British Columbia, respectively. Wolves were recolonizing our state on their own, perhaps using habitat corridors we were already committed to conserving!

The kids and I had been passing through the valley on vacation. Our timing was good to check on the Lookout Pack. The radio collar fitted to one of its adults indicated movement away from their natal den. At this less-sensitive stage, it was now okay for us to howl at them and listen for replies that might confirm the presence of pups.

The kids grumbled as we hiked the road, suffering mosquitos and heat. They may have figured this to be another of Dad's boring work forays. Then we reached our spot, and Scott let loose a big howl. In reply, the woods erupted in cacophony, including the yelps of pups too unpracticed to sound wolfy. Indelible in my memory are the looks on my daughters' faces as the moment switched from drudgery to nature's ultimate magic. I have been fortunate to see and hear wild wolves several other times, but this was the keeper.

If you were a wolf with a choice, Washington would be your best bet for a home. And if you were an informed admirer of wolves, you might note this as a testament to thoughtful collaboration. Yet for those in this collaboration, the wolf arena is more fraught than perhaps any other conservation challenge.

Washington wolves are killed by humans at a lower rate than those of any other wolf state except perhaps California, where wolves have only recently taken up residence. Where Washington has jurisdiction (e.g. outside Indian reservations), under four percent of our wolf population is deliberately killed annually by people, including lawful and unlawful incidents and by the state itself responding to livestock depredations. In Idaho, Wyoming, and Montana, as much as a third of the wolf population is killed each year, which is insane. Michigan, Wisconsin, and Oregon also see higher rates of wolf killing than Washington. In 2023, Oregon had a surge in wolf depredations on livestock, leading the state to kill sixteen wolves. Washington had a much quieter year and killed just two wolves. Similar numbers were recorded in 2024. Don't ask about Alaska or the Canadian provinces—you don't want to know.

These numbers reflect policy. Some states want few wolves, or none. Most authorize recreational hunting of wolves (barred in Washington except where tribal law allows), as their objective is to suppress wolves for the ostensible sake of livestock safety and/or to boost herds of big game for hunters. Yet research indicates that using recreational hunting to suppress a wolf population has little effect on the rate of livestock depredations or on the abundance of deer, elk, or moose. Ungulate population levels tend to be more influenced by factors like forage abundance, disease, and intensity of winters than by predation. On the other hand, research does indicate that reducing the size of large packs in ranching country can reduce local depredations on livestock, perhaps just by shrinking their number of mouths to feed. Sadly, politics tends to move management toward recreational hunts, ineffective though they are in relieving conflict with livestock, rather than the limited effort of targeting specific large packs for reduction in size.

We knew to expect the arrival of wolves even before the Lookout Pack showed up. Large wolf populations in nearby Idaho and B.C. made it inevitable. I directed CNW staff that our goal was for Washington to be where wolf recovery was done right. This at first fell to Jasmine, who was CNW's director of special projects at the time.

Jasmine and Derrick Knowles, who worked out of our Spokane office, engaged in a stakeholder process that the Washington Department of Fish and Wildlife (WDFW) convened to develop a wolf recovery plan in anticipation of their arrival. They did their job well. Then we campaigned effectively for public support to encourage the state's Fish and Wildlife Commission to adopt the finished state-of-the-art plan in 2011, shortly before all hell broke loose with wolf/livestock conflict.

In 2012, the BBC released *Land of the Lost Wolves,* a documentary about the return of wolves to Washington, featuring

Jasmine as the central figure. Its dramatic climax came when Jasmine and the film crew observed pups of the second pack to take up residence in the Cascades, in 2010 in the Teanaway Valley near the town of Cle Elum. The experience of traveling with this BBC team convinced Jasmine that our best approach to wolf recovery hinged on minimizing livestock conflict through deterrence practices, mostly using specialized cowboys called range riders. Wolves tend naturally to behave themselves, focusing on wild prey and ignoring livestock even in shared terrain. And with careful herd oversight through range riders and other means, conflict can be further minimized.

The essence here is that wolf management is about people. Wolves are reproductively fecund and are habitat generalists, meaning that we need not obsess about providing them habitat as we do with specialists like spotted owls. Wolves will thrive in a range of landscapes if they are not being actively persecuted with guns, traps, or poison. The path to avoiding active persecution involves focusing on factors that promote social tolerance and coexistence. Limiting livestock conflict is key.

Range riding is hard work. The riders must be trained, mounted, coordinated, and paid. They must be willing to put in long days away from home in summer and to find some other gig the rest of the year. A rancher needs to trust that this rider is familiar with his or her herd and their terrain, and that the rider won't be a distracting high-maintenance personality. Range riders have been used effectively for years in Montana, but at a limited scale mostly around Yellowstone. We wanted to model the practice here and needed a person of unique qualities to lead that effort. Fortunately, we had in 2009 just hired Jay Kehne, who fit the profile. He was hired to do outreach to farmers and ranchers for land conservation, but we shredded that job description and tasked Jay with leading a wolf field program. Jay is a Teddy Bear, much beloved in his Omak, Washington community. We hired him when he retired from a career in soil conservation with the Natural Resources Conservation Service.

In 2010, Jay and Jasmine worked with WDFW to offer a workshop in range riding in Colville, with experts from Montana presenting. Wolves were starting to show up in northeast Washington, and this was our chance to introduce the idea and techniques of range riding to the ranching community. Some reactionary ranchers took offense at the idea of coexisting with wolves, and they pressured WDFW to disassociate from the event. We proceeded alone and presented to a small group of just two families. This was a foretaste of the tough spot the wolf issue put us in, with ideologues on both sides.

After a year or two of hard work, Jay had recruited six ranching partners to pilot range riding, an effort CNW sustained for a decade. WDFW followed with a program of its own, providing riders to interested ranchers, but with a bit less dexterity than us. There has been enough drama and stress that Jasmine burned out and left in 2013. Derrick had already left to buy and publish a Spokane newspaper, which is apparently less stressful than conservation work in wolf country. By 2017, Jay too had become fried by wolf work, so we transferred him to other work. We quickly hired another Jay, this one conveniently surnamed Shepherd, who had until then been WDFW's key field rep for wolf conflict in northeast Washington. Shepherd's roots are ranching in southeast Washington and he, through his WDFW job, already knew even the toughest characters. Jay manages wolf stress more sustainably, perhaps by blowing off steam in a local soccer league, and he's in it for the long ride.

Range riding and conflict deterrence are imperfect. There will inevitably be conflict when wolves are around. Most wolf packs (perhaps 80 percent) behave themselves even without oversight.

If we do everything right, putting in maximum effort, we can get the peace rate to over 90 percent. That's how to minimize dead cows and dead wolves, as Washington is doing.

Here's the catch: On those rare occasions when, despite earnest effort by the rancher and range riders, wolves get a taste for beef, it's important to kill one or more wolves. It is the last resort, after first trying other tactics (fancy flagging, noise and light machines, rubber bullets) to shift the dynamic. Research indicates that killing a wolf quickly after a pattern of livestock loss can reset harmony. Otherwise, depredation can escalate to untenable levels to which the only remedy is tragic removal of the whole pack. The research I refer to here was a combined effort published in 2015 by multiple academic and agency biologists under the title "Effects of Wolf Removal on Livestock Depredation Recurrence and Wolf Recovery in Montana, Idaho, and Wyoming." Their analysis of years of data across these three states brings some confidence to their findings. But no doubt our understanding of wolves will continue to evolve. That is how science works, as a process more than a durable outcome or answer.

For instance, when wolves were reintroduced to the Yellowstone ecosystem, scientists observed changes in populations of prey (e.g. elk) and in the vegetative community, such as regrowth of aspen stands and streamside willows that in turn fostered increases in beavers and songbirds. This was heralded as a classic demonstration of what is known as *trophic cascade theory*, how the presence (or absence) of top-level carnivores has effects rippling through an ecosystem. Documentaries have been made about this Yellowstone transformation, told almost in the mold of a hero's journey, with wolves being the hero. This continues to make for great cocktail party conversation, telling how the fear of wolves changed how elk grazed, tipping ecological dominoes.

I can hardly think of any concept in ecology that I hear come up more frequently, generally stated as fact. Yet scientists do not consider the matter settled at all and continue to study and debate it. It is extremely hard to deduce hard truths about wolf behavior or impacts based on studies with sample sizes involving maybe a few dozen animals interacting in the widest and wildest parts of infinite nature.

One of our bleakest periods at CNW was our first experience with extreme wolf conflict. In the summer of 2012, the Wedge Pack was preying heavily on cattle belonging to a notoriously obstreperous rancher who had led the boycott of our Colville workshop two years earlier. WDFW took its first lethal action in early August, but incidents continued. By late September, wolves had killed or maimed perhaps dozens of cattle, and WDFW was under pressure to remove the pack. It was apparent that the ranchers had not conducted early deterrence effort that might have prevented this situation, so it was hard to blame just the wolves. But it was also apparent that if this carnage continued in news headlines, it could diminish public support for wolf recovery at a delicate time.

The agency director called to tell me that he was going to order lethal removal of the pack, and to ask if I would give a statement of support for the action. I saw in this tragedy an opportunity for progress and, through the director, negotiated this exchange of quotes in WDFW's press release:

> Jack Field, Executive Vice President of the Washington Cattlemen's Association, said, "We understand that as wolves re-populate the state there will be conflicts with livestock. We also understand that we need to work with WDFW to find solutions, including the use of non-lethal measures, in order to minimize losses for

producers, but we need everyone else to understand that managing and killing wolves that cause problems is an important part of a healthy co-existence."

CNW Executive Director Mitch Friedman said, "As difficult as this situation with the Wedge Pack is to accept on a personal level, we understand and agree that pack removal is the right action at this point. We have been strong advocates for exhausting all non-lethal means possible to avoid this situation and are extremely disappointed that it has come to this."

Other organizations saw a different opportunity, unleashing waves of press releases, action alerts, and fundraising appeals. One state senator told me that they received an average of four thousand angry emails whenever WDFW killed wolves. The name of the ranching family was widely reported in the press, and they claimed to have received harassing phone calls and even death threats. None of that outrage has helped wolves.

I believe in honoring social contracts. In this case, the social contract is between the wolf-loving public, which mostly lives in cities far from wolf action, and the rural communities among whom the wolves largely roam. Despite losing some friends, members, and donors, we stayed the course with our goal being to minimize depredations and wolf mortality by maximizing rancher buy-in on conflict deterrence, gradually demonstrating ever more peaceful coexistence. This graphic shows our success, I believe vindicating our choices.

Washington Wolf Recovery Compared to Other Western States in 2023

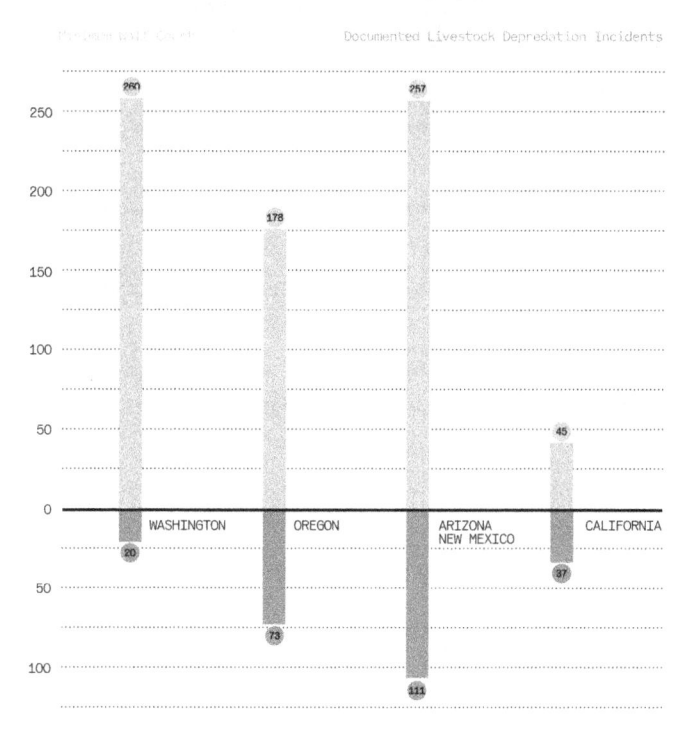

State	Minimum Wolf Count	Documented Livestock Depredation Incidents
WASHINGTON	260	20
OREGON	178	73
ARIZONA / NEW MEXICO	257	111
CALIFORNIA	45	37

There have been other depredation episodes in Washington, and the state has killed other wolves, including one other whole pack. But since wolves first returned to Washington around 2008, their numbers have grown to almost three hundred in more than forty packs occupying an ever-larger share of the state. And as ranchers incrementally commit to conflict-deterrence effort, the rate of incidents has declined greatly.

Even so, in the years following removal of the Wedge Pack, conflict and controversy remained high. Tensions were in the public, the legislature, and in WDFW's Wolf Advisory Group, which has diverse stakeholders, including CNW's representative, Paula Swedeen, PhD. Paula is CNW's policy director and for a decade has had perhaps more influence on Washington wolf policy than anyone. With advanced degrees in biology and economics, Paula served in positions within both Washington Department of Natural Resources and WDFW before switching to the nonprofit world. She has had a big hand in the state's habitat plans for spotted owls and other species and in its carbon policy. I tried a couple of times to recruit Paula and her big brain to lead our wolf program, finally bringing her onboard in 2014.

In 2015, WDFW brought in a specialized facilitator, Francine Madden, to undertake a method she calls Wildlife Conflict Transformation. Francine spent 350 hours interviewing over eighty people. Her method is basically counseling for political trauma, and listening is its essence. It worked pretty darn well here, and Paula is among Francine's biggest fans. But I think Paula herself deserves much of the credit. She has been tireless as a participant in the Wolf Advisory Group, in advising WDFW leadership, and in lobbying the legislature. A decade ago, wolf polarization was a massive distraction in Olympia, with wolf friends and adversaries each introducing combative bills to signal virtue to supporters. Paula, with help from a core group of invested legislators on both sides of the aisle, got them working in bipartisan fashion to fund WDFW's conflict-deterrence work. We have since not had many wolf-related junk bills to contend with.

Out in the field, we knew that some ranchers, including the family that was involved in the Wedge Pack and other incidents, were both skeptical of range riding and not really interested in working with CNW or even WDFW. Jay and Paula came up with an alternative approach. They drafted a bill that the legislature passed unanimously in 2017. It set up a way for the state, through its Department of Agriculture, to fund range riders via community-based nonprofits. Shepherd formed the Northeast Washington Wolf Cattle Collaborative with a volunteer board of community leaders. Since then, Jay's job at CNW has involved not only managing our few direct range rider pilot partners, which we have recently phased out of, but also hiring and managing about two dozen range riders through NEWWCC (Northeast Washington Wolf Cattle Collaborative) that he places with ranchers across that region.

Despite these efforts, wolf depredations peaked again in 2019, centered in the northern Kettle River Range. The Kettle Range is tough country for range riding, with rugged topography, thick forests, and thin grass. Cattle spread out there, contrary to the essence of range riding, which is to keep cattle bunched up, calves with their moms, and a human presence among the herd, especially at night. That all works better in open range than forested mountains. Rather than give up, we decided to give range riding a full test through a surge of effort. Paula and others persuaded the legislature to direct additional funds into the Kettle Range. So far, it has worked. In 2023, WDFW killed just two wolves, and those were in southeast Washington, outside of where our riders range. In 2024, there were again no WDFW lethal wolf removals in the Kettle Range. The credit goes not just to Jay's riders. Cattle Producers of Washington, a rancher trade association that is notoriously conservative, is now also funded (through the state program launched by the 2017 legislation) to place and manage range riders. In other words, the idea of deterring wolf conflict has now been accepted, if begrudgingly, by some of its most vociferous early resisters.

The benefits of this approach are less blood (both cow and wolf), more social acceptance of wolves, and less polarization.

This means there are fewer angry people inclined to secretly shoot or poison wolves.

We at CNW have achieved our goal of making Washington the place where wolf recovery is done right. The comparison to Oregon could hardly be more revealing. Oregon and Washington are similar in politics, geography, and status of wolf population. But Oregon's wolf advocates chose polarization over collaboration, so lawsuits outnumber range riders there. Washington had more conflict and wolf blood early on, as our program was building. But that has reversed. In 2023, Oregon had a mess of conflict and killed eight times more wolves than Washington. Their path forward is unclear.

When Oregon issued a report in April of 2024, showing that its wolf population had failed to grow, this was the public statement issued by one of the hardliner groups: "I anticipated this dismal report given the unprecedented increase in wolf-kill orders Oregon officials issued last year in response to livestock conflicts and the accompanying surge in poaching," said Amaroq Weiss, senior wolf advocate at the Center for Biological Diversity. "The science clearly shows that when states allow more legal killing of wolves, illegal killing also increases. Conservation groups have repeatedly raised this concern with the state wildlife agency, but they ignored us. Last year's population decline is the shameful result." I find it disturbing that she blames the state for the results of strategic choices made by her organization and its allies. I also find it unsurprising that she would claim scientific clarity where it does not exist.

Despite the evidence of the superiority of our collaborative methods, there are unremitting groups asserting a culture warrior approach here. They aim to undermine our progress by forcing Washington to adopt formal rules through which they could sue to obstruct lethal removal of wolves on those occasions when depredations are escalating and fast action is needed. The result would likely be alienation of ranchers who are invested in the present system. They also lobbied the Washington Fish and Wildlife Commission against reducing the legal status of Washington wolves from Threatened to Sensitive, which would have recognized that northeast Washington ranchers continue to struggle with the activity of the area's large and robust wolf population, even sometimes when employing diligent range riders. Some ranchers have more conflict than others. Some feel stress more than others with similar levels of conflict. Some have reacted to the situation by choosing to abandon agriculture, which puts their property at higher risk of conversion to housing and loss of habitat.

When wolf advocates fail to show awareness, if not empathy, for the realities of life in wolf country, they incite polarization that can diminish deterrence effort and end up increasing wolf mortality.

While a decade ago, it felt as though CNW's approach to wolf recovery faced cultural resistance from hardliners on both sides, it now feels like the holdouts are only on one side. It is conventional to describe that side as "to our left," but I see their tactics more as illiberal than progressive. It brings shame on the environmental community and adds to polarized discord in the nation.

I understand that some wolf advocates are so passionate that they don't engage from a strategic perspective. For them, this isn't about maximizing rancher buy-in or minimizing wolf/livestock conflict. Fundamentalists seek to impose rather than accommodate. Such people see CNW's approach as a sellout of some kind, and they project motives onto us.

For instance, we have been falsely accused of being funded by ranchers. Our wolf program has no agricultural supporters and costs us far more than it brings in. A sad fact is that donations flow more to those who maximize and exploit conflict rather than those who do the hard work toward enduring solutions. Those groups make money exploiting conflicts that we spend money trying to prevent. What is best for wolf advocates is not necessarily what is best for wolves.

It is natural for wolf supporters to wonder if there are not ways to advance recovery besides compromising and coexisting with livestock interests. Can we just pay ranchers for the cattle they lose? That is done, but the matter is more complicated than one might think. It is only a partial fix that is hard to implement, does not address the impacts that wolf stress may have apart from mortality, and does little to change underlying attitudes.

Can we ban cows from public lands? To whatever extent this goal is politically viable, it is risky to expect wolves to carry that weight. America has previously made the choice between wolves and cowboys, and I doubt the result would be better today than it was a century ago. It also would not address ample wolf conflict on private lands.

The best answer for both wolves and society is to try to meet everyone's interests through the hard work of mutual understanding, negotiation, and honoring of a social contract. Those of us who appreciate wolves can help fund through our taxes and donations programs that make wolf presence more tolerable for people impacted directly.

When Jasmine was filming with the BBC crew, they spent time in Alberta, Canada. While they ended up not using that footage in the documentary, something deeply meaningful still came from the visit. An Albertan rancher said to Jasmine, "I don't like wolves. But I know there are many Canadians who do like them. I respect those people, so I try to make it work."

Such grace binds democracy and sustains civilization.

9

Coexisting with Wolves

Range rider on the Colville National Forest
(photo by Chase Gunnell, courtesy of Conservation Northwest)

When we held our workshop on range riding in Colville in 2010, the one that the hardline ranchers boycotted, John Dawson and his son Jeff were in the room. We already had a relationship with the Dawsons. Two years before, during the 2008 recession, they needed help to make ends meet. Many ranchers are land rich and cash poor. When times are tight, they are forced to make decisions that can hurt their long-term interests and the land, such as overgrazing their grass or overlogging their woods. Worse yet, they might sell some of their valley-bottom land to housing developers. What the Dawsons did instead was to sell CNW a conservation easement to their land so it can never be developed.

We were happy to buy those development rights. Not only do we want to see agriculture sustained around rural communities like Colville, but this was a chance to develop a relationship with the Dawsons, who hold a permit to summer-graze cows on a wild part of the Colville National Forest, the Abercrombie-Hooknose Roadless Area. This beautiful high country should have permanent protection as wilderness. The Dawsons have mostly supported such a designation. What neither we nor the Dawsons foresaw was that our relationship would soon become about wolves.

The next summer, in 2009, the Dawsons lost a few cows to unknown causes. The matter became clear in 2010, when the presence of the Smackout wolf pack was recognized. Smackout Meadows, where that pack denned for most of the ensuing years, is a key part of the Dawsons' summer range, just south of Abercrombie-Hooknose. That's why they were in the room to learn about range riding. As John would say about their initial experience, "For a year or two, it felt like the wolves were managing my herd."

John and his wife, Melva, are down-to-earth folks on the cusp of their ninth decade of life. John was once a banker, making loans to ranchers. Their base ranch is just northeast of town. It's a modest one-story house on five hundred acres where they grow hay in summer and fence their cattle in winter. I have at times dropped by to visit their place when I am in the area, noting how new houses continually encroach on the fields along the road leading up to them. Melva tends a vegetable garden, as do I. Around Colville, you plant your peas when snow has melted from atop Old Dominion Mountain.

"We don't mind the wolves," says John, who has a naturalist's knowledge of the plants and animals in their area. "They're interesting to watch. But they do make life difficult for us at times. And I find it flustrating how the Wildlife Department works with us." I've heard John say "flustrating" a hundred times and still don't know whether it is deliberate.

Their daughter, Leisa, does most of the wolf work. She was our most consistent range rider. Her summers are spent atop a horse or ATV, minding the herd. A typical day starts with trying to learn where the wolves are from rumors and radio collar data when WDFW is willing to share it. The rest of the day and maybe part of the night is spent up with the herd, trying to keep the peace. That alone is a big change from before wolves returned, when some ranchers might leave their cows to their own established patterns until they, as autumn chill set in, walk themselves back to the home ranch. Having people up with the herd strikes me as a good change, irrespective of wolves, and a return to cowboy traditions. But it's a big labor cost that eats into thin margins for ranchers who have seen the cost of land, fuel, and feed skyrocket over the years, even as global trade has kept wholesale commodity prices (beef, lamb) flat. We helped by paying a share of the range rider cost, and by lobbying the state to fund the program that matched our contribution. I also have helped a bit by selling Dawson beef to Seattle friends and neighbors who were happy to pay retail price directly to the family for beef they knew was raised humanely.

All that is fine and sustainable. But then the wolves act up.

While the Dawsons have been the most diligent ranchers in practicing wolf-conflict deterrence, there is some drama almost every year. They might lose a calf or two without warning. At times, when the pack is acting surly, they may need to rally the family for overnight shifts at Smackout Meadows. A few times, we at CNW recruited staff or volunteers to camp out with the Dawson herd until the wolves backed off. Our staff, Jay Shepherd, probably stashes a toothbrush up there.

A few times, the depredations added up enough that, despite all the diligent effort, WDFW took appropriate action by killing at least one wolf to disrupt the behavior.

The costs mount for the Dawsons. They were initially ostracized by some in their community for working with us and presumably validating that wolves were not simply to be killed as earlier generations had done. I have seen the Dawsons after sleepless nights and spoiled summers, the pastoral quality of their ranching life diminished to a memory. And I have seen them at their wits end dealing with the state bureaucracy, trying to get their invoices paid, wolf location data, or conflict response in a timely way.

The Dawson experience is neither unique nor typical. The Gotham family, for instance, grazes their herd in rugged national forest of the southern Kettle Range that has been roamed by several packs for the past dozen years. They too have been consistent in posting range riders, and I have signed a lot of checks to their son, Logun, for his range riding. But the Gothams experience far less wolf conflict and drama. I can't say whether the difference is the terrain, the wolves, or something else.

Part of the difference might be personality, as Bryan Gotham is prone to taking life calmly in stride, seldom flinching. Jay and Paula were once with Bryan out on the range, as they were giving a tour to a couple of CNW donors interested in learning more about wolf-conflict deterrence. They stopped to look at some fresh wolf tracks that Bryan had seen earlier beside a forest road, evidence of focused activity by several rather large wolves in close proximity to Bryan's cattle. Jay described the eyes of the donors widening with the sudden realization that here the appearance of tranquility rides a knife's edge against turmoil. Bryan was nonplused, and the tour continued without much being said.

If backcountry predators fail to fluster Bryan Gotham, I know what does. The city. Around 2012, we had an important meeting that required Bryan and his wife, Deb, to come to Seattle. Despite them having grown up in eastern Washington and Bryan having spent part of his military service at Fort Lewis, just south of Tacoma, they had always avoided the city itself. Their discomfort with traffic or something meant that I had to meet them at the highway exit and escort them in.

Difference in personality, however, is not the whole distinction between the Gotham and Dawson experiences. It is also evident that the Gothams' lives have been affected by wolves far less than the Dawsons despite how close to one another their homes and pasture ranges are. I think of wolf drama like weather—a tornado might ravage one property and leave neighbors unaffected. It is not a big deal until it is. At least wolf drama can, unlike weather, be partly deterred.

Do absolutist wolf advocates know what life can be like in wolf country? Do they care? I am not sure. Wolves are not demons, and they should not be demonized. But neither are they gods to be deified. They are amazing and beautiful animals that live in complex social units and play big roles in ecosystems. We want and need them on the landscape. But they can also be a pain in the ass, and to keep them around we must give help to folks who live and work among them. Doing so allows the chance that nature can bring us together instead of further polarizing us.

10

Better Beef

Dawson family cattle, Smackout Meadows
(photo by Chase Gunnell, courtesy of Conservation Northwest)

On a crisp October day in 2022, Jay Kehne and I were hunting deer on the Figlenski Ranch, in northcentral Washington's Okanogan County. This special place means a lot to me for reasons I will explain later. There is little more exhilarating to me than autumn hunting in the Okanogan. The air is still with cold mornings and warm afternoons. Aspen and cottonwood leaves have turned yellow and orange. With luck, I will cross the scent or sound of deer, sparking something primal and arousing all my senses. If so, I will consider it a successful hunt irrespective of whether I get off a shot from my Remington 30-06. A great hunter I am not, and I am fine with that. If I don't get a buck in the Okanogan, which is almost assured, I can notch my deer tag and fill my freezer with one from an island of Puget Sound, where deer are grossly overpopulated in the absence of predators. Killing an island deer is an ecological and social service.

The Figlenski Ranch is about ten thousand acres, or fifteen square miles of almost entirely open country. We start before dawn, finding a good prospect on the ranch's eastern margin, in the mid-valley of Tunk Creek, which tumbles due west into the Okanogan River. We sit with binoculars and wait, hoping emergent daylight will reveal a mule deer buck. When the sunlit scene disappoints, we rise and walk slowly west and downhill, exploring terrain that is entirely new to us. Eventually, we approach the property's western boundary, where brush-lined ravines offer a good place to flush a white-tailed deer. But no such luck. From here we look down into McLoughlin Canyon, site of a large river-fronting property rich in cultural and ecological value that, like Figlenski Ranch itself, CNW recently helped put into the ownership of the Colville Confederated Tribes.

No deer that day, but we marveled at what we did see: magnificent terrain and healthy bunchgrass and sagebrush. No fences, no litter of spent beer cans or ammo shells. Not even many cowpies or tracks. This land has been grazed by cattle for well over a century yet is in great shape. We had a near wilderness experience on a cattle ranch. That is rare in Washington.

Cows have a heavy hoofprint on the American West. They are native to much wetter European ecosystems and are responsible for grievous impacts like muddied streams with eroded banks, diminished fish populations, depleted soils, weed-invaded grasslands, absence of native dung beetles, interrupted fire cycles, and even atmospheric methane. Beef clogs American arteries. The cows themselves are often abused in industrial operations where they are crammed together, fed corn they cannot properly digest, and deprived of any free and natural life.

They also taste great and are almost certainly here to stay.

Despite decades of activist efforts to remove cows from public land for the sake of clean streams, wild wolves, and even the federal budget (fees to graze cattle on public land are a fraction of those charged for private land), little has changed. Sisyphus never tires of pushing this boulder uphill, but I am open to alternatives. While public lands produce less than two percent of the beef Americans consume, these are among the limited free-ranging and grass-fed cattle preferred by conscientious consumers who hold concerns about their own health and the humane treatment of livestock. Grazing cattle on mountainous federal land in summer allows ranchers to use their private valley bottom land, otherwise vulnerable to housing development, for growing hay to get them through winter. So, if cattle are not to be banished, what can we do to make their presence more compatible with landscape conservation?

You have already read about how ranching can coexist with wolves. That is critical, as the last time America chose between cows and wolves, the latter was exterminated. I find it unlikely they would win a political rematch. You have also read about how CNW, like other conservation groups, have used tools like easements to perpetuate ranches for societal benefits including both agriculture and wildlife habitat. In many places, cattle grazing is one of few economic uses of the land. When a cattle ranch dies, its most likely successors are houses.

What if there was technology that allowed ranchers to greatly reduce their harmful impacts while reducing costs? That is what virtual fencing offers.

Our first test of virtual fencing involved the Figlenski Ranch. When we bought this ranch for the Colville Tribes in 2022, Mike Wilson had been leasing grazing rights from Ernie Figlenski. Mike wanted to continue his lease, and the Colville Tribes were open to that. Jay Kehne had recently heard about virtual fencing, and he arranged a partnership for this to be Washington's virtual-fencing pilot project through a company called Vence. A 2015 wildfire had burned up much of the ranch's fencing, the rebuilding of which can cost up to ten thousand dollars per mile. Avoiding that cost gives great appeal to any alternative way to confine cattle.

Virtual fencing makes use of existing cellular signals relayed through dedicated towers strategically placed. It also uses a computer app and collars on the livestock to enable a rancher to easily and cheaply "fence" cattle on preferred pastures. The fence is a line drawn in the app. As a cow approaches that virtual line, she hears a beep that escalates in tone until it shifts to a mild shock. Mike found that some of his cows were more prone than the rest to cross through virtual fences. He prioritized these for butchering. Evolution in action!

This technology allows one to quickly and easily fence cattle away from streams and sensitive habitats. If a wolf pack establishes a den within your range, just use the app on your phone or PC to draw a new fence around the den, keeping cattle a safe distance away and reducing the risk of conflict. The same is true for, say, breeding sites of sharp-tailed grouse or sage grouse. It costs nothing to keep cows out of an area for a day, a month, or forever.

Virtual fencing also makes it cheap and easy to concentrate cattle grazing in a particular location. Cheatgrass is an invasive weed that has taken over much of the American West, spread mostly by cattle. During much of the year, it is inedible and highly flammable, extending our wildfire problems. But in spring it makes for tender forage. Using the app, a rancher can now focus his cattle on eating down this noxious weed during those few palatable days. We may therefore find that virtual fencing can reduce weeds, revive native grass, and help restore more natural wildfire conditions.

Virtual fencing can also help maximize carbon stored in soil, keeping it out of the atmosphere and mitigating climate change. In certain soils and climates, grasses and their roots thrive if they are grazed and trampled aggressively for a short period, then allowed to rest and regrow for a year. A rancher can efficiently accomplish this using fenced paddocks near his home, but certainly not on sprawling summer range in the mountains. With virtual fencing, such rest and rotation is now possible and being tested.

All this gives virtual fencing appeal. But here is what most excites me: It renders obsolete much old barbed-wire fence. This means we can remove it and restore the open landscape for free-roaming wildlife as it was before the stringing of the Devil's Rope, as Indians of the day called it, a century and a half ago. Imagine the West without barbed wire! You may live to see it.

Virtual fencing has so many benefits in stewardship and labor-saving cost reductions that it is spreading like, sorry, wildfire. Our initial pilot effort with Mike Wilson cost CNW under forty thousand dollars to erect three repeater towers on appropriate high ridges, which relayed signal coverage to over sixty thousand acres of range. Mike pays an annual lease for each collar, one for every cow. (Collar technology is evolving rapidly, making short-term leases more practical than purchase.) Mike and his wife, Joy, have been enthusiastic evangelists for the technology within the ranching community. In the two years since, use of virtual fencing has spread to use by twenty-seven different ranchers on over one million two hundred thousand acres of Washington. CNW has helped get towers in place on National Forest in the Methow Valley and on Puget Sound Energy's Wild Horse Wind and Solar Farm near Ellensburg, Washington. With Jay's help, we are also seeing uptake begin in adjacent areas of Canada.

I have heard from skeptics. I know an Okanogan County rancher who lost miles of fence to the Pearl Hill Fire in 2020. Assuming (probably falsely) that his ranch was too rugged for virtual fencing, he secured hundreds of thousands of dollars in federal disaster relief to rebuild. I kept my mouth shut, but that story made me an unhappy taxpayer. Another rancher I know thought the expense of collars was too high. When we probed about that cost relative to replacing fences, the disturbing reply was that their herd ranges without fencing. This means that streams and other natural features are paying the cost.

In June of 2024, my team helped organize Washington's first virtual fence conference, which brought about 150 attendees from the agriculture community together in Wenatchee. Early in 2025, Jay will join the Wilsons on a virtual fencing panel before a Spokane audience of two thousand ranchers and range-management professionals. If one's goal is to eliminate cattle from the landscape, this is all bad news. If one's goal is to improve the landscape while offering rural communities a chance to prosper, the news could not be better.

11

Hunting for Solutions

Author hunting on Figlenski Ranch
(photo by Jay Kehne)

Jackie, who would become my wife, and I were going out to buy a piglet. This was in about 2010, when my daughters were in their early teens. We were not actually going to take home the piglet, just confirm that she was being treated well by the family on Bellingham's fringe that had posted the ad on Craigslist. If so, we would leave a deposit and return months later to take delivery of butchered pork.

I invited Jessie and Carrie to join us, surmising that they would enjoy the outing and seeing a cute piglet rooting about. They were instead appalled. "Why would we want to meet something that we are going to eventually eat?" For years I had been feeding these girls venison from deer I had shot and butchered, bison or beef bought from trusted ranchers, and eggs from chickens and ducks in our yard. All of this was intentional. I called the question: "Would you rather eat meat from an animal that you had enough relationship with to know had a good life, or one you had no connection to and could assume its life had been miserable?" Their answer, if I remember precisely, was, "Duh!" Apparently, the emotional world is more important than the living details of livestock.

My daughters were young, so they can be excused. But I really don't know how the average American would answer that question. I do know my own answer, contorted though it is. I do not like shooting the deer I eat, though I continue to do it. If I had the opportunity, I would shoot an elk but not a moose or a bear. I have killed and butchered, with zero pleasure, roosters and ducks that I had raised. I infamously and regretfully did the same with a turkey that made the mistake of landing in my chicken yard.

My ethics around hunting and indeed eating are admittedly inconsistent. They slip further when it comes to the marine fish, squid, and clams that I like to harvest, process and eat. (I have largely given up fishing rivers and lakes.) I readily photograph and even post to social media my clam haul, but never that of a deer I killed but do not want to disrespect.

The point is that ethics are tricky things. I know and admire people who live vegan lifestyles that are intentionally as light on nature as possible. I also know and admire people who hunt and are every bit as ethical and deliberate about their relationship with nature as those vegans.

Sadly, not all hunters are so noble. I have heard countless hunters display openly an attitude that implies that paying their license fee entitles them to wild game, as though nature is a vending machine. If the topic is wolves or cougars, many hunters will vent about competition, even ranting about the bloodlust of wolves that supposedly kill just for fun, leaving dead quarry to rot. Such opinions are not limited to white hunters, as I have seen them on tribal social media including from people I know and value.

One could argue that hunters are among both the best and worst people in the woods, both the most and least attuned to nature. They run the gamut from expert backcountry archers to road poachers. American hunters have organized themselves into interest groups for over a century. These groups have a history of impressive impact on policy, including conservation. Hunters and anglers lobbied to generously tax themselves to fund regulatory agencies and habitat measures to protect the resource their interest relies on. Under the Pittman-Robertson Wildlife

Restoration Act of 1937, eleven percent is added to the purchase of guns and ammo, which the federal government distributes to the states for things like research on wildlife and land acquisition for habitat. Tens of billions of dollars have been raised and spent over the century. Congress passed a similar law, the Dingell-Johnson Sport Fish Restoration Act of 1950, to tax fishing gear to fund protecting that resource. There is no comparable added tax on backpacks, fleece, and binoculars to support maintaining hiking trails, not to mention stewarding the birds and animals that motivates many into the backcountry. Nor is there a tax on mountain bikes to pay for their needs or impacts.

Hunting groups range from fire-breathing conservatives to almost liberal. Such groups have been part of the coalitions behind just about every campaign that has ever persuaded Congress or a state legislature to protect a wild place.

It is tempting to want to impose ethical limits on hunting. But whose ethics? As I confessed, mine are a mess! It is often people who have the least direct knowledge and experience who try to set the standard. At what point the effort crosses a line into counterproductive culture war is hard to say. But there is such a line, and it gets crossed often.

CNW helped pass a voter initiative about twenty-five years ago that outlawed certain wildlife-trapping methods in Washington. Reduced trapping has been a benefit to wildlife conservation, including the recovery of fishers and wolverines. Yet we have since relied on trappers for wildlife conservation and had great experiences doing so. CNW collaborated with the National Park Service, Washington Department of Fish and Wildlife, and others to reintroduce Pacific fishers to the Olympic and Cascade Mountains. One of our roles in that effort was paying and coordinating with trappers in British Columbia and Alberta who provided the animals. Dave Werntz did that work. Dave also worked substantially with trappers from Kelowna, British Columbia, in our work with Tribes and First Nations to restore lynx to northeast Washington. (More about these successful efforts later.) The trappers were knowledgeable, helpful, and generally thrilled to get income trapping for wildlife restoration rather than pelts. We could not have achieved our goals without them, so I am glad that they exist. I have also read in government surveys the heartbreaking statements of remote British Columbia trappers complaining that rampant clearcutting of boreal forest had eliminated their quarry and livelihood. These people, many of them Natives, were the human voice of the forest.

CNW was also involved in a voter initiative in 1998 that banned certain hunting practices, including the use of bait to attract bears and use of hounds to pursue bears or cougars. Our motive was to reduce the chance that hunters using these practices would inadvertently harass or kill grizzly bears of the fragile and then-dwindling North Cascades population. One result of that initiative is that even today, few cougars are killed in Washington using dogs, which are now restricted to problem situations (when a specific cougar is acting in ways considered risky to a community). A lot more are killed by boot hunters, meaning somebody who is hunting for deer or other game when he has a chance encounter with a cougar. It is legal for that hunter to shoot the cougar if he has an inexpensive endorsement on his license. It is a common occurrence. Even I once engaged with a cougar while he and I were both pursuing deer. I had no interest in shooting that cat, preferring to revel in observing him through the scope on my rifle. The upshot is that now more cougars are killed than prior to the initiative.

Another result of the initiative is that the state put a lot of money and effort into studying cougars. There is quality research indicating that mature male cougars (called toms) tend to be well-behaved. They silently go about their deer-hunting business. Some fitted with radio collars are found to be living and hunting amongst human homes, passing through backyards undetected and without mischief. These toms also defend their territory against young cougars, which are less well-behaved. If the tom is killed, the young delinquents move in, often followed by rising complaints about vanished pets, or cougars seen too close to the schoolyard or bus stop. Those complaints pressure wildlife officials to allow more cougars to be killed, which can extend the negative cycle. (Though Bart George, a Spokane-based biologist working for the Kalispel Tribe, has done research showing that cougars can be effectively hazed from an area, responding more if the hazing involves dogs. The prospect of non-lethal deterrence is very welcome.)

Boot hunters are usually not selective. They shoot the cougar that crosses their path, generally with no knowledge of its sex or age. Hound hunters are generally more expert and may also have a good view of the cat that their hounds have treed. The hunter has the option of shooting only younger or female cougars, letting the big toms go. Ideal would be if cougar hunting was limited to selective hunts using hounds. But ideal is hard to achieve.

Most people agree that it is ethical to hunt deer and elk for food, particularly in a place where they are abundant. Can the same be said about hunting cougars? Is it ethical if the hunter eats the cougar's meat, as is often done, and unethical otherwise? The same questions could be asked about hunting of black bears, which are numerous in parts of Washington. Some Indians hunt and eat black bear while others have spiritual reasons not to. This might vary not just between Tribes but between clans or even families. Some Indians hunt cougars and wolves under the specious belief that doing so bolsters game populations for subsistence hunting by Tribal members. None of these are easy questions.

I subscribe to *Northwest Sportsman Magazine*. I am not interested in the articles on hunting tales or techniques or even the wild game recipes. I like its editorials, which I find to reflect solid conservation values. And I like the feature report on poachers that have been busted by state officers. Hunting has traditions and a culture in which poaching is widely condemned. Were it not for the strong culture stewarded by these organizations and publications, poaching might be more common. A would-be poacher probably cares far more about being ostracized by those he can relate to than by those whose culture he already feels alienated from.

One of the biggest problems facing wildlands today is motorized recreation. Some people with powerful vehicles (trucks, ATVs, etc.) drive them on creek beds, across delicate meadows, and in other places where they damage habitat and disturb wildlife. There are organized clubs of people who enjoy four-wheeling, though these groups tend to not be as large, old, or established as hunting organizations. Laurel Baum, on the CNW staff, has found she can partner with motor recreation clubs on some projects, including restoring streams or habitat damaged by rogue riders. The people who belong to such groups tend to be more law-abiding and are aware of the harm that illicit riding causes to the land and to the reputation of their hobby. But many people who own these expensive and powerful vehicles have not grown up in a responsible culture and are not associated with a group that fosters one.

A collaboration I undertook with motor recreationists left a bad taste in my mouth. Along with a friend who represented a sportsman's group, I negotiated with a few leaders of the motor clubs a deal whereby all-terrain vehicles would have easier access to roads in exchange for a requirement of visible license plates and higher infraction fines. The idea was to facilitate more legal riding but less unlawful (harmful backcountry) riding. Our leaders in the legislature were a liberal Democrat and a conservative Republican who troublingly later emerged to be a leader in a Far-Right militia movement. Our bill passed unanimously and remains state law. The bad taste comes from the dishonorable actions of those we collaborated with, who immediately and unilaterally returned to the legislature to try to sweeten their deal. Worse yet, rural sheriffs and prosecutors turned out to have little interest or capacity for engaging on the enforcement provisions, so we failed to reduce the harmful actions of the bad apples.

I wish motorized recreation groups had as much history and culture as the hunting groups, and that rogue riders were ostracized to the same degree as wildlife poachers. Maybe someday that will be the case. The bottom line is that while there are hunting practices that rub me the wrong way, I see hunters as allies and partners, sharing the big tent of conservation. I would hate to see culture war push them away from us.

Part III

Conservation Principles

12

Forests and People

James Johnston cutting a slice from a giant stump
for display in 2004
(photo by Jasmine Minbashian,
courtesy of Conservation Northwest)

In the chill dark of a tropical night, Barbara Dugelby and I sat at the top of Temple Number 5, the second highest in the ruins of the Mayan city of Tikal, in northern Guatemala. The glow of a faint moon afforded me a landscape view so I could imagine the workings of the city that had declined eleven centuries earlier. A fog rolled in to envelope the ground and forest below us, leaving visible only the pyramidic peaks of a few temples appearing to hover in the sky. Accentuating the eeriness were the guttural barks of howler monkeys rising from the shrouded woods and the sense of ghosts from what was, at its peak, among the world's most densely populated cities.

We had the privilege of night access, alone in this biosphere reserve, by virtue of Barb doing her graduate research there. She had been a fiercely effective leader of Earth First! in Texas before her graduate study focus. I was visiting for a couple days while exploring Guatemala for my 1992 winter vacation. Barb guided me around the ruins and explained her studies. I recall looking at where excavation had exposed a living cross section of time. The ruins of the lower part of a temple had been partially cleared, exposing its steps. The transition between excavated and not was stark, exposing the vertical face of several feet of intact soil from which grew trees of a seemingly ageless rainforest reaching for the sky. I marveled at the sequence. I have seen desert places in the American Southwest and in Israel where the ruins left by people well over a thousand years ago are barely changed. The jungle is less forgiving. A single millennium had seen forest not only conquer this once-vibrant city of stone, but so completely overwhelm it with generations of verdant growth that unexcavated human ruins appear as forested hillocks.

I struggled to comprehend time in this context. Civilization had ruled this land, receded for reasons we still do not understand, and was then authoritatively consumed and buried by the inexorable forest. But wait, how could these ruins be old when I know standing western redcedars in the Northwest that were alive while Tikal still bustled? I have also seen bristlecone pines in California that sprouted in the early Bronze Age, almost five thousand years ago. It is beyond me to reconcile the discordant time scales of human and forest history, not to mention geology. Yet forests have had a profound influence on humanity and the rise and fall of our civilizations. One factor in what we inaccurately refer to as the "collapse" of the Maya may have been repercussions from their having deforested their landscape.

Other ancient civilizations collapsed for reasons clearly tied to shortsighted exploitation of the woods. *A Forest Journey: The Role of Trees in the Fate of Civilization*, by John Perlin, is a detailed trove on this subject. Perlin details the rise and fall of societies from ancient Mesopotamia to colonial New England, and how they ravaged forests for heat, shipbuilding, metal smelting, to expose arable land, and even in acts of war to deprive adversaries of timber to meet these same needs. Demand exhausted supply until society collapsed. Cyprus rose and fell, then rose again a half-millennium later after its forest had regrown. Then it fell again.

I think we are doing better these days. My forest activism has been driven not by aversion to logging, reverence for trees, or fear of deforestation and societal collapse. My concerns are more practical than apocalyptic. Nature itself is hard on trees and forests. They burn and blow down in storms. It is natural for there to be temporary gaps in the canopy and in the forested landscape. It is also reasonable for people to use trees to make useful stuff. The devil is in the details.

I was once deputized to guard the nest of a spotted owl family for a weekend. I may even have been paid for the work, though I can't quite recall. This was in the late 1980s. Biologists had learned of this owl nest within the boundaries of a logging operation on state public forest in Washington's Olympic Peninsula. The logging had been ordered halted. The same thing had happened the previous summer in a nearby stand, leading to owls being bludgeoned by vigilantes. My weekend assignment, requested by friends in the Department of Game, was to prevent the recurrence of that tragedy.

I was in a surly and reckless mood due to a breakup with my girlfriend, Beth. My drive out to the forest had me following Highway 101 around the northern perimeter of the Olympics, a landscape scarred by logging. The massive clearcuts offended me, as they had done Franklin Roosevelt when he toured the Peninsula in 1937. He is reported to have remarked to a congressman at his side, "I hope the son-of-a-bitch who logged that is roasting in hell." As I approached the town of Forks, the self-proclaimed logging capital of the world, the spirit of FDR possessed me to stop in at the Forest Service office there. I demanded to see the district ranger, an infamous timber beast. While waiting in the lobby, my blood rose as I gawked at wall photos that glorified the logging of great forests.

The ranger, a towering man, came out accompanied by a subservient forester and asked what I wanted.

With wildness in my eyes, I barked, "I heard about your logging holocaust. I see now that what I heard is all true. I hope you burn in hell for what you've done to these forests!"

They remained calm as the forester clasped his hands in front of himself and stated matter-of-factly, "Well, you're certainly entitled to your opinion."

I turned and resumed my journey to the owl nest.

Getting there required that I drive through the battered landscape of the Hoh-Clearwater State Forest, in tatters from two decades of relentless logging. The stand in which the owl nest persisted poked out like an island in a hilly sea of stumps. I drove the logging road into that stand, welcoming the shady relief from July heat. It was mid-afternoon, and I set up camp. At some point, I made the call of a spotted owl and succeeded in bringing the family to me, where they perched on nearby branches. Two adults and two fledglings. Calling owls was something one could do in those days but dare not now, as it exposes them to risk.

The following morning, I became aware of the distant engine rumbling from a large pickup truck. Oh shit, I thought. Here we go. But instead of a group of angry loggers, this turned out to be an agency truck carrying three biologists. Along with my two friends from the Department of Game, there was Eric Forsman, a young Oregon scientist whose graduate studies had revealed the decline of spotted owls and their dependence on old-growth forest habitat. Forsman delicately cocked his head to one side and adeptly offered a set of hoots that melted the hearts of owls near and far. He gently captured the young fledgling owls by use of a mouse and a modified fishing rod. I got to hold one of the weightless softball-sized puffballs as Forsman fitted an identification band on its legs before releasing it back to its family.

I don't know if the northern spotted owl will survive more than a few more decades of competition from its invading cousin, the barred owl. The causes of that invasion include human actions that made habitats more suitable for barred owls, facilitating their arrival and flourishing in the Northwest, at the great cost to other species even beyond spotted owls. Barred owls are a bit bigger, more aggressive, and eat a wider variety of prey than their cousins. Some of those prey species are themselves rare. Federal managers are trying to give spotted owls a chance by killing barred owls in strategic locations, such as the Olympic Peninsula, where the geography may lend itself to influencing owl demography. It is gut-wrenching, though.

I do believe we have done the right thing in trying to save spotted owls, and that the Northwest Forest Plan represents good science and policy irrespective of whether spotted owls make it in the long-term. A whole array of species rely on old-growth, from small mammals and songbirds to unique insects and lichens in the canopy and critical fungi in the soil. Amphibians and fish, including salmon, thrive in cool, clear water that drains slowly from an old forest but can be unleashed in muddy torrents from clearcuts. The epic forests of the Northwest are also champions at storing carbon, keeping millions of tons of it from causing climate mischief in the atmosphere. Still, the Herculean effort did center on trying to balance the future of the owl with that of the region's timber towns, yet both have suffered worse than expected. The causes of both declines (owls and timber towns) include important ones that are beyond the policy and practices of the Northwest Forest Plan, but the results are fitting for a Shakespearian tragedy.

We need both healthy ecosystems and an abundant supply of wood, a miracle resource. Thank goodness we not only know more about forest ecology than did the ancient Mayans and Mesopotamians, but also more about forest practices. I believe logging can be done sustainably. The first step is protecting enough of the old forest to meet the needs of dependent species and streams. I am not opposed to clearcutting as a method in particular forest types, such as Douglas fir that require direct sunlight to regenerate. But I am not a fan of industrial efficiency in forestry, whereby the clearcut is quickly replanted with seedlings that are protected from competing brush with herbicide, then the cycle is repeated just a few decades later. This is a shortcut to exhausted soils while depriving us of habitat, carbon storage, and even timber jobs.

Much better results are attainable if clearcutting is delayed until the trees are at least eighty years old. By that time, they can provide myriad ecological and atmospheric benefits. Meanwhile, loggers can extract useful logs by thinning the stand. We at CNW have conducted modeling that shows this approach producing as much timber volume as the forty-year rotation, without even a temporary shortfall. Further, the logs include larger ones suitable for a greater variety of wood products. There are forests managed this way by public agencies and even private companies. The downsides from a corporate perspective include that the work is more labor intensive (jobs!) and could extend the period of risk of wildfire or regulatory change. But mostly it is a matter of maximizing short-term returns to stockholders.

That sensible forestry does not align well with the demands of Wall Street provides a strong argument for much more forest acreage being owned by the public, Tribes, or even nonprofit organizations funded by philanthropists. The returns on investment are compelling, including massive amounts of carbon stored, improvements in wildlife habitat, public recreation access, and more jobs to perhaps rejuvenate ailing timber towns. Nobody would burn in hell for treating our forests in this way!

Better forestry is enabled by improved technology. Modern mills use lasers to guide precision cuts and glues to turn remnants of small logs into big, strong pieces of lumber with little waste. The number of mills today is a fraction of what it was in the 1980s, but these fewer mills process a similar amount of timber, of course with far fewer workers. Many towns no longer have a single mill, and the ones that remain are highly automated. We can meet our needs for forest products and habitats without deforestation.

There are big risks to forests besides forestry. The conversion of timberland for residential development and agriculture is one. Washington lost over seven hundred thousand acres of forest this way in just the final quarter of the twentieth century. Climate change is another, as coming decades will see forest ecosystems reassembled as the ranges of each tree species shift. We already see this happening. Some places now forested will before long be unable to grow trees, at least of the species we are used to there. It breaks my heart to see western redcedars dying in my region, likely due to climate. Intact old forests will withstand climate changes better and longer than young forests will. This is another reason that the Pacific Northwest should be envied and emulated for its conservation of old-growth forest.

It is likely that carbon stored in trees and other natural features will continue to be increasingly valued in financial markets. If our economy made sense, we would also build into prices the dollar value of all the services nature provides, from clean water to wildlife. With carbon serving as a partial proxy, standing forests can be valued beyond just what conservation philanthropists are willing to donate toward them.

13

What Muir and Leopold Got Wrong

John Muir, circa 1902
(public domain image)

Until about age forty, my strongest attachment and sense of purity and justice was to wild nature. A corkboard in my childhood bedroom was pinned with a collage of postcards I had collected, all of nature scenes. Where a road or powerline corrupted an image, I covered it with green marker. Life was binary: natural or human, with the former good, and the latter tarnished. I might have been a bit extreme in this, but I don't think I was alone. Love of nature runs deep in the American psyche.

"Climb the mountains and get their good tidings," wrote John Muir in *The Mountains of California*. "Nature's peace will flow into you as sunshine flows into trees. The winds will blow their own freshness into you, and the storms their energy, while cares will drop away from you like the leaves of Autumn."

His beautiful words carried insight and inspiration. They motivated the nation and its leader, Theodore Roosevelt, and catalyzed America's national parks and nature preservation movement. Muir founded the Sierra Club in 1892 to apply his philosophy to the land. While many of his contemporaries saw nature as dark and hostile, Muir espoused its majesty and benevolence. For all this, we owe him much.

Muir's hometown was Dunbar, on the Scottish coast. My wife, Jackie, and I visited Dunbar in 2023. We walked its gorgeous trail named for Muir, admiring the seabirds. We toured the house, now a museum, where he lived until the age of eleven, when his family moved to America. It was easy for me to see how nature in this stunning setting captivated and molded Muir. It set him to evangelize for wild nature and against the ravages of early industrial society.

"The clearest way into the Universe is through a forest wilderness," Muir wrote. He had much right—but not all. While forests may have felt to him like wilderness, that was in cases a dangerous illusion that haunts the minds and actions of nature lovers to this day.

You'll find the tell in this next quote, from Muir's diary of his summer of 1869 (published in 1911 as *My First Summer in the Sierra*): "Along the main ridges and larger branches of the river Indian trails may be traced, but they are not nearly as distinct as one would expect to find them. How many centuries Indians have roamed these woods nobody knows, probably a great many, extending far beyond the time that Columbus touched our shores, and it seems strange that heavier marks have not been made. Indians walk softly and hurt the landscape hardly more than the birds and squirrels, and their brush and bark huts last hardly longer than those of wood rats, while their more enduring monuments, excepting those wrought on the forests by the fires they made to improve their hunting grounds, vanish in a few centuries."

Muir apparently did not understand that Native Americans had already been decimated by disease and persecution that began over a century before his observations. What he saw in the later years of the nineteenth century was a faint remnant of their presence on a landscape they had stewarded substantially since at least the last ice age. Estimates of the pre-contact population of California range from a few hundred thousand to over a million. We probably will never have a clear idea. But by the time of Muir's writing, Indians in California had been reduced to maybe twenty-five thousand, under five percent of their historical presence.

There is strong evidence of humans in western North America dating back at least fifteen thousand years and potentially twenty-three thousand years, if the dating stands of human footprints found in New Mexico's White Sands National Park. The impact of early Natives was likely nominal during the glacial period, but they spread and grew in numbers and impact as the climate allowed. Their effect became for a while more brutal than harmonious, as they altered naïve ecosystems and may be implicated in the sweeping extinctions of Pleistocene megafauna. Many of the wildlife icons we associate with wild America and Canada today—deer, elk, moose, cougar, gray wolf, black bear, grizzly bear—were minor then. The Pleistocene landscape featured instead mammoths and mastodons, tiny horses, camels, sloths, and ferocious carnivores. Dire wolves and short-faced bears were genuinely badass, as were big cats like American lions, sabretooths, and cheetahs. These animals shaped and roamed landscapes that we would hardly recognize. When the big elephants were gone and no longer maintained northern grasslands with their grazing, boreal forests grew up in their place.

Theories abound on what caused the demise of these species, but its coincidence to the expansion of Native people is unmistakable. It is unlikely that human hunting alone triggered such a collapse. A recent hypothesis is that Indian fire transformed the landscape to that which the modern fauna is better suited. This seems plausible, as people would discern the benefits of fire for opening sightlines, reinvigorating soils, and boosting forage for game. "The fires they made to improve their hunting grounds," as Muir wrote. What Muir described as "wilderness" was an illusion. The fires "wrought on the forests" by Indians were in many ecosystems the defining feature of Native presence for over ten millennia.

At first, the fires would have been a devastating shock to nature, transforming the vegetation and associated wildlife, driving dozens of species to extinction. Whether one considers humans of that period as natural or even wild is academic—the landscape and ecosystems evolved accordingly. By Muir's time, many types of forest depended on fires ignited and/or encouraged by Indians to remain healthy and "natural." That the features looked wild to him was because disease and persecution had recently diminished generations of Indians and their practices.

This all came as a revelation to me when, around 2003, I read Timothy Flannery's *The Eternal Frontier: An Ecological History of North America and Its Peoples*. My worldview and activism had stood on a false foundation of the notion of a timeless North American wilderness, a land of wolves and grizzlies in which Native Americans were another compliant feature of the landscape. I was wrong. Much of the nature I was fighting to protect was associated with forms of human stewardship that predated agriculture by several millennia, replacing what had endured here for previous millions of years.

What did *wild* mean in this context? Together with several colleagues who also read Flannery's book, I really struggled with this.

Muir's hostile view of fire came to dominate, especially after the Big Burn of 1910 swept through millions of acres of the Rocky Mountain West. The young U.S. Forest Service was given a clear mandate to fight fire, initiating the reign of Smokey Bear. Forest fires were suppressed rather than promoted in America. (Canada has a related but distinct history.) Similarly, exclusion of fire (and the decimation of bison) also changed the Great Plains, enabling eastern cedar trees to encroach over millions of acres of grassland. Of course, industrial scales and methods of logging and farming also emerged throughout this period to further transform the landscape, but my point is about the myth of supposedly pristine wildland. What kept the land in ecological health, able to support its contemporary wildlife, was fire, much of it deliberately set by people. University of California researchers published in 2007 that, "Approximately 1.8 million hectares (a hectare is about 2.5 acres) burned annually in California prehistorically (pre-1800). Our estimate of prehistoric annual area burned in California is 88% of the total annual wildfire area in the entire U.S. during a decade (1994–2004) characterized as "extreme" regarding wildfires." A 2019 study done by a group of researchers from The Nature Conservancy and the University of Idaho made similar findings. "We document that only one-tenth of the area expected (through modeled historic fire regimes) to burn in the forests of Washington and Oregon did so over the last three decades."

In other words, America before European contact saw an extent of wildfire that makes today's pale in comparison, though the frequency of those fires meant that they were generally far less intense. The 2019 study found that over a third of acreage burned in the past three decades did so at high intensity, whereas historically (before European contact) less than ten percent did. It was mostly good fire, widespread every year.

Which leads us to Aldo Leopold, a hero of mine. Leopold was the father of wildlife management and decades ahead of his time in understanding ecology. In 1935, he helped found the Wilderness Society to advance protection of wildlands. His essays, published posthumously in 1949 as *A Sand County Almanac*, remain some of the best writing on nature. (My copy is an award I received, inscribed by Aldo's daughters, Nina and Estelle.) But like Muir, Leopold did not account for the extent of Indian influence in healthy American ecosystems.

In his essay titled "Wilderness," he famously describes wilderness as "a base datum of normality, a picture of how healthy land maintains itself as an organism." He went on: "Paleontology offers abundant evidence that wilderness maintained itself for immensely long-periods; that its component species were rarely lost, neither did they get out of hand; that weather and water built soil faster than it was carried away. Wilderness, then, assumes unexpected importance as a laboratory for the study of land-health."

That essay mentions Indians only once, in the context of comparing rivers of the Southwest to "similar rivers in the Sierra Madre of Chihuahua, never grazed or used for fear of Indians . . ." Say what? If white settlers avoided the Sierra Madre for fear of Indians, it means that the Indians were using it. The question is how intensively and for how long?

There were parts of North America less used or altered by Natives. Extreme deserts, swamps, and mountains presented environments not suitable for much more than transit by humans. Similarly, the Douglas fir forests of western Washington and Oregon are wet and dense, making them less prone to modification at large scale. Though there is recent research from western Oregon indicating that burning (likely cultural) was more frequent than previously believed even in these forests. Nonetheless, I think it is reasonable to apply to such areas the concept of wilderness, defined in American law as areas "untrammeled by man." But elsewhere, the concept is confounded by the historic intensity of Indian use and modification, mostly through fire. Ecosystems that co-evolved with Indian practices during those twelve thousand or so years would, in the absence of fire, experience changes that are not necessarily desirable.

Perhaps Muir and Leopold should have known better. Muir did mention Indian fire, but in the context of it being an insult to the land. Leopold mentioned Cabeza de Vaca, the Spanish explorer who was one of four survivors of the 1527 Narváez expedition who were traded among Tribes from the Florida Panhandle all the way west and south to safety with Cortez in Mexico City. How could Leopold have read de Vaca's account without recognizing the ubiquity of Indian presence in its descriptions of pre-colonial, pre-epidemic landscapes? How could it have been "wild?"

My intent is not to judge but to adapt. The philosophical fathers of American conservation greatly underestimated the extent of Native human influence on ecosystems, and they therefore overstated the ubiquity of what is today commonly considered wilderness. Generations of romantic writers and conservation campaigners have been inspired by, and infused with, this errant thinking. The result is that progressive doctrine romanticizes both Indians and wild nature without reconciling the relationship of the two. I certainly did as a young activist. But what I have learned since is more complex. Nature wasn't a big wilderness before the Pilgrims. While there were wilder pockets in the harsh environments of the mountains and deserts, most areas were actively managed by Native Americans.

The past few decades have seen much published in academic literature about Native presence, stewardship, and practices, including fire, but less so in journals of the conservation and wilderness movements. The turn of the millennium saw an interesting flurry of publications on the validity of the wilderness concept. Dan Flores, in his 1999 book, *Horizontal Yellow*, has a strong treatment of wilderness in the context of Native history, including fire. Charles Mann published in 2005 his book *1491*, which presented the ubiquity of Native presence and practices prior to the arrival of Columbus, though it was light on the topic of fire. In contrast, Dave Foreman, a wilderness evangelist and cofounder of Earth First!, generally gave short shrift to Indians or fire in his speeches and writing. You will find no such mention in Foreman's 1999 essay titled "The Real Wilderness Idea," in which he defended the concept from intellectual attack (on philosophical grounds) from particular academic writers.

In 2013, Dave wrote this in his online blog, *Around the Campfire*: "As I stumble beyond forty years in the fight for wild things, I've come to believe that conservation boils down to how far and deep Man's will should spread over Earth . . ." Dave cited earlier scholars and etymology to reach his favored definition of wilderness as "self-willed land." He went on: "This self-willed-land meaning of wilderness overshadows all others. Wilderness means land beyond Man's will. Land beyond Man's will is a slap in the face to the arrogance of humanism—elitist or common man, capitalist or socialist, first worlder or third—and for the new *über*arrogance of the Anthropoceniacs; for all, it is also something to fear." I can buy into that for the more rugged and remote places I have already described as having not been subject to thousands of years of Indian fire and substantial presence. But those ecosystems that were subject to heavy Indian presence and frequent burning were really not all that self-willed, even if they could still be considered "wild" and of characterizing "wildness," two terms that I see as sitting towards one end of a gradient of human management. I think highly of these terms and of the term wildland. I also very much love wilderness, as a term, concept, and place. But I believe that it should be applied only where it fits.

It is still common today that discussions of forest and wildland conservation will romanticize the wild state of the precolonial landscape. But consider that the native population of the Americas before Columbus is now estimated to have been between fifty and one hundred million, with large cities and extensive agriculture. The population was so large, and having such an extensive impact on nature, that its collapse due to deliberate genocide and associated epidemics starting around 1500 led to a rebound in forested acreage so extensive that at least one group of scientists hypothesize it was a cause of the planetary cooling known as the Little Ice Age. This means that while the precolonial American landscape was "natural," it was not what we today think of as "wilderness." And fire and smoke were ubiquitous. This was the case for over ten thousand years.

Proponents of wilderness persist in disregarding the role of fire in ecological health. Many organizations push to protect from active management as much public land as possible, irrespective of fire ecology. I have even recently heard interviews with, read articles by, and even had written exchanges with, old conservation friends and leaders in which they have continued to show this flawed logic, ignoring the role of Indians and their extensive fires in the pre-contact landscape. One could call out the social injustice of that neglect, but that is not my point here. It is ecologically ignorant and harmful to ignore the role of fire, amplified by the practices of Native peoples, in maintaining many ecosystems. This does not mean that fire-dependent forests should be clearcut. It does mean that they are likely ecologically unhealthy due to fire suppression, and that they may benefit from restorative management, including at least fire, possibly preceded by careful thinning.

The binary model—wild or not wild—has dangerous allure, like Homer's song of the Sirens. The still-prevailing notion is that more natural is mo' better, with wilderness being best. We now know this contrast to be often false and harmful to fire-dependent ecosystems. It can also foster sentiments of misanthropy. I have felt those myself and read or heard them expressed by many nature lovers over the years. But while I can think of good reasons for misanthropy, there is little basis for the view that human presence is novel or that wildlife and nature would be pure if altogether free of it. We need a clearer picture of what wild means, where it is the right standard, and what alternatives to apply elsewhere.

Leopold himself provides my preferred answer in "The Land Ethic," his final essay in *A Sand County Almanac*: "A thing is right when it tends to preserve the integrity, stability, and beauty of the biotic community. It is wrong when it tends otherwise." For ecosystems located beyond the substantial influence of humans, wilderness meets that test, and we must keep such areas as wild as possible. But for those areas adapted by thousands of years of substantial human influence, the passive wilderness approach is likely to reduce integrity, biodiversity, and arguably even beauty. In the absence of periodic low-intensity fire, dry forests become overgrown and grasslands less-productive or replaced by trees. Wilder is not better in such areas. This does not justify abuse; the Land Ethic still applies. What management is indicated must be resolved, especially now that climate change has altered fundamental conditions.

14

Land and Wildlife Management by Native Peoples

Dixon Terbasket and his daughters, Nicola and Reiley
(photo by the author)

"The big old trees aren't there anymore," said Mike Allison, an elder and council member of the Upper Similkameen Indian Band (USIB), based in Princeton, British Columbia. "I used to visit and spend time with these trees. They had great meaning to me. So many have been cut down. I would go to visit an important tree and find a stump."

Mike was crying and making me cry. A slight-bodied chain-smoker, Uncle Mike, as his community knows him, is more soulful and earnest than anyone I have ever known. He is somebody you want to be helpful to. I'm afraid I have not been as helpful to him and his beautiful but suffering valley as I would like, not that I haven't tried.

I was introduced to the valley of the Similkameen River in 1994, while campaigning for Cascades International Park. I received a call from Glen Douglas, an elder of the Lower Similkameen Indian Band (LSIB), whose territory is just downriver from that of Mike's band. The Similkameen River drains the northeastern portion of the North Cascades, forested at upper elevations and arid lower down where it flows among grasslands, orchards, vineyards, and the fruit markets of Keremeos. Glen was calling to ask me about environmental assessments that might help his band resist the expansion of a ski area on land they claim as traditional territory. He invited me up for a sweat lodge ceremony and introduction to his people and homeland.

The sweat was traditional, but honestly not the experience I had expected. The other participants were white military veterans. Glen himself was coping with trauma from World War II, Korea, and Vietnam. He had fought for the U.S. in all three and returned home to the Similkameen Valley for his sunset years. Glen introduced me to Dixon Terbasket, a Native leader who worked then as manager for the LSIB. Dix and I have been brothers since. We had our respective daughters at about the same time, shared marital challenges and separations in common, and have shared many days hunting deer. He even indulged me through an awkward karaoke phase. Dixon's mother, Theresa Ann, is the eldest elder in the community and has been generous in sharing cultural legends and more with me.

My invitation for the LSIB to support the international park didn't get far, but we stayed in touch. The Similkameen Valley became a treasured place for me. The big window in Dixon's kitchen looks southwest to Snowy Mountain, which is just north of the border from the Loomis Forest lands we protected in 1999. There was a push then to designate seventy thousand acres around Snowy Mountain as a provincial park to protect it from logging. The LSIB opposed the proposal, both because the province had trouble respecting the rights and title of First Nations, and because the LSIB and its members gained jobs and revenue from logging. I got myself on the agenda for a meeting of their Chief and Council in 2000, hoping to find some agreement to protect Snowy Mountain.

Crossing the border into Canada has not always been easy for me due to my arrest record. On this day, I was denied entry and had to attend the LSIB council meeting by phone. The council was gracious, maybe even amused. I suggested that the economy was changing and that the Band had an opportunity to protect their cultural and natural heritage without losing prosperity. I pledged that CNW would invest to help. We had funds leftover from our Loomis Forest fundraising efforts, enabling me to commit two hundred and fifty thousand dollars to the LSIB toward such things as studies in ecological forestry methods and ecotourism, new tech for their office, and a new headquarters building.

Today, Snowy Mountain is a protected area, and the LSIB has a beautiful building with design features from their Native traditions, but there remain a great many challenges. Excessive logging continued in the watershed, impacting the temperature and flows of the river. A century of mining left toxic legacies, and active mining upriver near Princeton threatens not just more pollution but possible failure of two towering earthen dams that store the viscous waste from decades of mineral processing. A breach would wipe out the valley for generations. For thirty years, I have worked on these and other issues with the LSIB and lately their USIB cousins. I love these people. I know their leaders and many elders, and I feel absolute gratitude for how they have allowed me to be part of their community.

Dixon is a bit of a badass. He was a teenager in the mid-1970s, when the American Indian Movement was fighting for Native rights in the U.S. He helped Leonard Peltier, the famous leader of the American Indian Movement, escape across the Canadian border to hide out in an LSIB neighborhood. Most Indians I know have strong views on tribal sovereignty and rights. But Dix, being charismatic and forceful, has made a name for himself. When he and I flew to Haida Gwaii in 2008 to learn how the Haida Nation co-manages and benefits from Gwaii Haanas National Park Reserve, it was less than an hour before Dixon was recognized in town. Soon after, we were invited before the Skidegate Band Council and provided a guide.

I have done a lot to help the Similkameen Bands, but Dixon has told me that I have not done enough. If Dixon had his way, probably all First Nations and Tribes would be more direct in pursuing their interests. Other leaders take different views on the matter. The path forward is not obvious, though in Canada, it is now better illuminated.

The Supreme Court of Canada ruled in 2014 (Tsilhqot'in Nation v. British Columbia) that First Nations with title have the "right to the benefits associated with the land—to use it, enjoy it and profit from its economic development." First Nations often have title (and therefore rights) far beyond land that is covered by treaties, which are few in Canada relative to the U.S., where treaties are numerous and continue to have (as they should) the full force of law on reservations and often well beyond. After centuries of gross mistreatment, Indian Tribes have not only survived but are generally resurgent, as argued by David Treuer in his excellent 2019 book, *The Heartbeat of Wounded Knee: Native America from 1890 to the Present*. In general, U.S. treaty Tribes have larger reservations and have rights that are more clearly defined, while First Nations in Canada have broader rights and title to larger traditional territories that are still being defined in law and practice.

What can we expect of land management by Tribes and First Nations? I think it will be an improvement, coming closer to that of Leopold's Land Ethic than that of non-natives.

My friend Lauren Terbasket, an LSIB leader (but not a direct relative of Dixon despite them sharing a common LSIB surname), told me that Indians no more want to be romanticized than infantilized. They are people, like all of us. An Indian operating a chainsaw or bulldozer in the same way as a white will have the same effect on the land. I certainly have seen Tribes and individual Indians make resource management decisions that I disagree with. The prospect of better decisions and practices comes not from skin color, DNA, or any assumed aversion to capitalism, but from distinctions in culture and governance.

I have Indian friends who are committed to, and skilled at, resource conservation despite not having had a traditional upbringing or being particularly spiritual. I know other Indians who are somewhat indifferent to wildlife except for its use in hunting, focusing instead on the business of materially benefiting their people. I know still others who are highly spiritual, steeped in culture but not in ecology. And I know Indians fully learned in what is called Traditional Ecological Knowledge, or TEK, that unites cultural and ecological wisdom.

Braiding Sweetgrass by Robin Wall Kimmerer is masterful in describing TEK and its complex relationship to Western science. I believe in TEK and have been privileged to know some practitioners of it. Mike Allison of the USIB is such a person, as is Chief Rob Edward of the LSIB. Both have been generous in sharing their knowledge with me. Chief Rob decries how the land has changed due to both poor management practices and the absence of cultural fire, meaning fire set by Tribes in keeping with traditional practice. In many places, food plants no longer grow. And because Indians and grizzly bears eat many foods in common, Rob says, "If there isn't food for the grizzly, there isn't food for me."

Science is not the only "way of knowing" that can have validity. There is much genuine knowledge and wisdom handed down through generations in place. But let us also be candid about the challenges to TEK. Even in the most remote places, Indian communities have been disrupted by the traumas of disease and brutal oppression for well over two centuries. Their languages and cultures have been suppressed. Some Tribes were forcibly moved far from ancestral homelands to confederate with others that do not share their ancestry or culture. What degree of TEK can we expect to have been successfully passed down through this gauntlet to today's practitioners?

An added challenge is that the land is not the same as in ancestral times. Local ecosystems have been ravaged by industrial extraction, invasive exotic species, and climate change. I think it is likely that for many Tribes and First Nations, TEK itself is often in need of restoration. Leaders should know that they can't, for instance, resume burning forests as their ancestors did without first considering the present condition of the land and whether the skills of the TEK Keepers remain sharp after generations of having been prevented from practicing cultural burning. But we do know that they are fully motivated to resume their role and have much knowledge on which to build.

Tribal governments have additional challenges. They are under pressure to provide employment and sustenance for their people, often on marginal lands that the U.S. government chose to push them onto. For many Tribes, their lands are also distant from centers of commerce and the economic opportunities associated with them.

Given all these challenges, what makes me optimistic that tribal resource management will come closer to Leopold's Land Ethic? Kinship culture. In his book, *The WEIRDest People in the World: How the West Became Psychologically Peculiar and Particularly Prosperous*, sociologist Joseph Henrich reveals how distinct are people he labels as WEIRD: western, educated, industrialized, rich, and democratic. Most cultures across time and the planet are characterized more by kinship than the individualism that developed in Protestant England and spread throughout its empire.

When you have relationships with people in Indian communities, you find they spend far more time than the average Westerner in ceremonies, often funerals. Their communities are like large extended families. It is true that many Indians leave home to live and work outside their community, just as non-

Indians do. But tribal governments are mostly comprised of, and influenced by, those who stay and are committed to the long-term interests of the Tribe and its homeland. Most tribal governments consist of an elected council and chair or chief. While this structure is more colonial than ancestral, councils may still be influenced and constrained by more traditional power centers, such as elders, matriarchs, and TEK Keepers. They generally work hard to protect and provide for the subsistence interests of their members, whose hunting for meat and gathering for food and medicinal plants is both cultural and practical.

Another cultural element of tribal governance is its law. Many Tribes and First Nations have laws governing themselves and visitors to their territory. These laws may be based within cultural stories or teachings and have different ways of operating than Western law. They are likely to be rooted in principles of nature and its stewardship, such as reinforcing that relationships with nature and its beings should involve respect and reciprocity, even seeing plants and animals as relatives. This motivates Indians and their governments to restore native species to their lands. CNW has partnered with Tribes and First Nations to recover grizzly bears, lynx, sharp-tailed grouse, and other wildlife. The Yakama and Colville Tribes have each reintroduced pronghorn antelopes to their respective territories. It can get more complicated with large carnivores like grizzly bears, wolves, and cougars, as not all Indians or Indian governments fully embrace their presence.

Here is an example of how traditional story influences tribal law and how it affects policy. It involves the Enloe Dam, which blocks the Similkameen River a few miles before it flows into the Okanogan River at Oroville, Washington. The dam is on the traditional territory of the LSIB. There have long been calls to remove the dam to help salmon runs. The LSIB formerly opposed removing the dam, which sits amid a natural rockfall that partially blocks the river and is the subject of a cultural story. That story says that Coyote, or snk'lip, caused the rockfall in ancestral times out of anger at the band for depriving him of a love interest. Snk'lip threatened bad consequences if salmon were to get above the falls. For this reason, the LSIB opposed efforts to gain salmon access upriver, including dam removal. Since the LSIB are of the larger Okanagan (or Syilx) First Nation, and the Okanogan (different spelling on each side of the border) are in turn one of the twelve Tribes of the Colville Confederation, dam removal was also long-opposed by the Colville Tribes.

The LSIB's position on dam removal changed in 2008 when, under the leadership of Chief Rob Edward, they studied the snk'lip story more closely. The story recognizes that some salmon and steelhead did get above the rockfall. These fish were sacrosanct, not to be harvested. Their presence was a test of the people's will to follow Coyote's law. Chief Rob changed the LSIB's position to be in support of dam removal but only to restore the pre-dam river, with the rockfall remaining as a partial barrier to salmon passage. I helped arrange meetings between leaderships of LSIB and the Colville Tribes to communicate this change, bringing about a shift in the Colville position as well. The Colville Tribes are now actively pursuing dam removal, which hopefully will be done within a few years. Climate change is elevating summer temperatures in the Okanogan River to levels harmful to fish, and the cool mountain waters of the Similkameen, once free of impoundment, will help offset that.

It is exciting for me to see numerous U.S. Tribes request from the federal government designations of national monuments within their territories. I have the same feeling about Canadian First Nations that declare Indigenous Protected and Conserved Areas within their territories, and the efforts of the British Columbia government and various conservation groups to arrange community-based financing to support and assure intended implementation of such protected areas with perpetual income to the First Nations. These efforts are modern attempts to blend Indian legal rights and culture with U.S. and Canadian land management law. Each proposal is distinct, with varying degrees of co-management, protection of cultural and natural resources, restoration of traditional place names, and other objectives. President Biden, in his goal of protecting 30 percent of America's lands and waters by 2030, included and embraced these tribal-led approaches and established through presidential proclamations several large new national monuments, mostly in the Southwest. We are seeing the evolution of Indian-led resource management before our eyes, and it is high time. Working with Tribes and First Nations to support them gaining their rights and improving land and wildlife stewardship is another way that conservation groups can indirectly pursue our goals. But doing so requires a lot of humble learning and long, careful, patient, respectful engagement.

The interplay of culture, tradition, and practicality involves management decisions that may be surprising to those on the outside but are within the rights of sovereign nations to make. For instance, the Colville Tribes now have a robust gray wolf population on their reservation, with seven or so active packs. The Colville Business Council authorizes unlimited hunting of wolves by tribal members, a policy not popular with some biologists, including me. Their objectives in allowing hunting of wolves include promoting cultural practices, which is great, but also helping game populations. Given that their reservation has very healthy numbers of wolves, deer, elk, and moose, their current hunting rate of ten to twenty wolves per year is probably having little if any effect on those ungulate populations or on the ample success rate of subsistence hunters. Still, plenty of tribal members would be happy to see far more wolves killed, if the opinions I have seen shared on the Tribes' Facebook are indicative.

So, do the Colville Tribes favor wolves more or less than the general population of Washington? The answer is clear as mud. Similar complexities come into play in tribal relationships with cougars, whales, and forest practices. The relationship of Indians to wildlife and the land may upset an animal rights or anti-logging absolutist. But as sovereign nations, they have the right to manage as they choose. And I believe that over time, they will tend to come closer to meeting the standards of Leopold's Land Ethic than most white governments.

15

Helping Government Succeed

The author releasing a fisher in
Mt. Rainier National Park in December, 2016
(photo by Paul Bannick)

One prominent environmental group boasts on its website that "83 percent of our lawsuits result in favorable outcomes," and they promise "more no-holds-barred action." I used to make similar claims until we at CNW found ways to have impact on the ground rather than in courts and media, where wins often do not translate into benefits for wildlife. We search for solutions we can manifest. We measure progress in outcomes that help nature and communities. We even help government agencies to efficiently fulfill their conservation missions.

In 2001, shortly after our success saving the Loomis Forest wildlands, we had surplus funds from that campaign even beyond the quarter-million dollars I committed to the Lower Similkameen Indian Band. We decided to explore reintroducing Pacific fishers, a large furbearing member of the weasel family that aggressive trapping during the Great Depression had reduced to extinction in Washington. We granted sixty thousand dollars to the Washington Department of Fish and Wildlife (WDFW) to study the feasibility of reintroduction. From this grew a twenty-year collaboration between us, WDFW, and the National Park Service that successfully reestablished self-sustaining fisher populations in the forests of the Olympic Peninsula and the North and South Cascades. Our roles, managed first by Fred Munson and then Dave Werntz, included raising and managing grant funds with which we paid trappers and veterinarians in British Columbia and Alberta to provide the three hundred or so fishers that were released.

One of my most gratifying days was in April of 2020, when WSDOT cameras filmed a fisher using an I-90 wildlife underpass. This momentously signaled that we had sufficiently reconnected the ecosystems of the North and South Cascades—by both protecting forested habitat corridors and catalyzing construction of wildlife crossing structures—that the fishers we had reintroduced were able to now interbreed and maintain one large, viable Cascades population.

These and other efforts resulted in relationships with motivated scientists working within multiple agencies. Around 2006, Jen Watkins and Joe Scott hatched the idea of convening these friends to discuss habitat connectivity and carnivore recovery. This became an annual event called WildLinks.

You've met Jen a couple times, but I am only now introducing Joe. When I hired him in 1998 as our conservation director, Joe had been working as a Volvo mechanic in Seattle. He had been on the CNW board of directors for several years, displaying incredible conservation passion and knowledge. Raised on the mean streets of New Jersey with an accent to prove it, Joe was caught up in the rebellious 1960s while attending Boston College. Lean and irascible, Joe appears taller than he is. My toddler daughters called him Big Boy Joe. His own sons were adults by then, giving him the flexibility to move to Bellingham and take a pay cut to pursue his passion for grizzly bears and wild nature. His curmudgeonly charm and transparent dedication have helped him to serve the critters well. Renowned wildlife biologists have grown to trust and deeply collaborate with Joe despite his lack of formal science education. Some people even call him The Bear Guy. It didn't hurt that Joe could use his mechanic's skills to keep our auto maintenance costs down. After a quarter-million road miles had exhausted the battery on the CNW Prius, Joe replaced it in his driveway.

We hosted the initial WildLinks conferences in modest locations like the lodge in British Columbia's Manning Provincial Park and in a First Nation's RV campground in Osoyoos, B.C. Attendees share research and progress, and together cook up new plans. It grew over the years to become the favorite annual gathering for stalwarts enjoying time with compatriots and the shared fulfillment of on-the-ground projects. People found these meetings to be reviving and empowering.

We never formalized WildLinks. There are no agency guidance documents, interagency agreements, or turf squabbles —just peer-to-peer relationships and open sharing of information and ideas. From it grew such collaborations as the Washington Wildlife Habitat Connectivity Working Group, itself an *ad hoc* interagency effort that has conducted modeling that makes Washington perhaps the best-mapped jurisdiction in North America for wildlife corridors. Lynx are returning to Washington's Kettle River Range through a collaboration (between CNW, the Colville Confederated Tribes, Okanagan Nation Alliance, and Upper Columbia United Tribes) that was hatched in WildLinks sessions. When grizzly bears are restored to the transboundary North Cascades Ecosystem, hopefully soon, some of the credit will belong to relationships formed and discussions held at WildLinks.

At its essence, the formula is simple: people with shared conservation interests partnering to efficiently make the world better. Attendees include motivated staff of state, provincial, and federal government agencies with wildlife, land, and transportation missions, along with academic, tribal, and conservation NGO folks. What we have learned together is that conservation progress can be the result of organic relationships. People just getting stuff done together without lobbyists, lawyers, new policies or laws, or polarizing campaigns.

I consider this—citizen groups helping the functions of government—to be another form of indirect tactic. This is a curious turn of phrase, as it seems like organizing everyone to work together toward a common objective is more direct than the so-called *direct actions* of protest, but whatever. I do distinguish the indirect tactic of helping government to succeed from the forest-restoration and wolf-recovery collaborations I described earlier, which focus on finding common ground with other civilian stakeholders that government can then hopefully act upon.

Both are, of course, very distinct from the direct approach of reflexively battling government agencies. Yes, that is sometimes necessary, and CNW has sued the government plenty of times. But the cumulative effects are disturbing. Many activists and organizations demonize the agencies and officers of government as adversaries, targeting them with rhetoric, protests, and lawsuits. This is so common that it seems normal. A reason is bound up in the origins of our environmental movement. In 1965, Ralph Nader published *Unsafe at Any Speed*, about the failure of federal agencies to properly regulate the auto industry. It touched a nerve, and Nader responded by catalyzing a whole movement of nonprofit organizations with activists and lawyers to hold public agencies accountable. Groups like Natural Resources Defense Council were born. In his book *Public Citizens*, Paul Sabin chronicles that history, putting it into broad context. Nader's movement was entirely new, pivoting from America's general trust in government and industry to distrust and adversarial oversight. This was warranted, just as it was twenty years later when activists like me took on the Forest Service for transferring public forest wealth to the timber industry. But as Sabin reveals, there was no plan for later restoring public faith in government agencies. Now, sixty years on, some continue to battle with, and communicate regarding, government agencies as though they are enemies rather than instruments of the public. I think this has taken a serious toll in how Americans view government. A 2024 Pew survey found public confidence in the federal government down to just twenty-two percent, a drop of fifty-five points since the mid-1960s.

I have been a witness to, and a participant in, what I consider kneejerk litigation, where the objective is to obstruct and delay. It has made me wonder what life is like in less-litigious cultures in different places and times. Here and now, we seem to file suit simply because we can. Frequently, the arguments raised in these lawsuits are based in procedural rather than substantive law. In other words, it is not a debate over whether the proposed project will, for instance, pollute water or harm protected wildlife, but just whether the public agency has not done enough study or sufficiently invited public comments. It is seldom clear that the procedural hoops lead to better environmental outcomes, while unintended outcomes include bloated government budgets, agency leaders too risk-averse to execute their mission, citizen groups trained to mobilize and empower NIMBY (Not in My Back Yard) sentiments, and the fact that even good government projects (restoring overgrown dry forests, reintroducing native wildlife, building mass transit) are preceded by redundant thick studies driven less by informing a quality decision than insulating it from lawsuit. The added costs in time and money mean we have a government that is less efficient and responsive, contributing in the big picture to public cynicism. I would support thoughtful modifications to environmental policy statutes, though I fear that the Trump Administration will push to go way too far. We should have reformed the laws when Democrats were in power, though that would have been considered apostasy by many of my colleagues.

It is better that environmental proponents show restraint in using the courts, and instead engage upfront in collaborative work that signals to agencies what solutions and decisions are best supported. How can we expect our agencies to be strong and trusted enough to protect our resources when we continually disparage them and chip away at their credibility? "Trust is foremost among the social virtues that make healthy societies," wrote Eric Liu and Nick Hanauer in their book, *The Gardens of Democracy: A New American Story of Citizenship, the Economy, and the Role of Government*. The Forest Service was once proud and deservedly respected. It lost its way, ravaging our forests for the timber industry until we appropriately forced a correction. But now, when we need the agency to be strong enough to restore our forests to climate resilience, its staff is thin and demoralized. I once heard that the most popular screen saver (when that was a thing) in Forest Service offices was a clock counting down minutes to retirement.

Similarly, while there are reasons to criticize Washington's Department of Fish and Wildlife, it is overseeing the nation's most successful wolf recovery. Yet some advocacy groups attack it as a scofflaw, with volume always up to eleven. Is this because they flatteringly hold Washington to a higher standard or because they mine rich Seattle for donations? Whatever the case, there are reporters and activists who now have the unjust belief that Washington has the worst wolf recovery record rather than the best. This may even inhibit other states from adopting Washington's successful model of deterring conflict between wolves and livestock, thus perpetuating the cycle of violence that wolves suffer.

Another positive example of helping government function involves WDFW, which state legislators had come to treat as a neglected stepchild. The department was an easy target, being politically isolated between competing interests. Hunters want more game. Animals rights activists want less hunting. Conservationists want carnivores. Everybody fights over salmon policies and harvest quotas. These and other interest groups each appealed to their friends in the legislature, which interpreted the fray as the sign of a failing agency. The legislature withheld funds, worsening the problem. By 2018, WDFW not only had a deepening budget hole, but legislators were blaming the deficit on the agency itself. The result was a funding bill that directed the agency to undergo an audit and convene a stakeholder oversight group, to which I was appointed.

I expected the stakeholder group to be acrimonious, with, for instance, clashes between hunters and nonhunters. Instead, we found unanimous support for the agency's stated mission "to preserve, protect, perpetuate and manage fish and wildlife and to provide fishing and hunting opportunities." When the external audit vindicated the agency's fiscal management, it became clear that the job of us stakeholders was to send a unified overarching message of support to legislators while pursuing our competitive agendas more tactfully. This we did, and the legislature quickly restored the department's budget.

A continuing problem with WDFW is that its spending is overwhelmingly related to hunting and fishing, with biodiversity getting the smallest slice of the pie. We were able to reach agreement within the stakeholder group to fix this. There were only two options: One was to reallocate funding to biodiversity from the programs that serve traditional constituencies (hunting and fishing), which would instigate distracting backlash. We chose instead to grow the overall pie and enlarge the biodiversity slice of it. Efforts to find a new source of revenue (such as taxing sales of hiking gear, as has long been done for hunting and fishing gear) did not get far in the legislature, so we have settled for increases of state general funds.

Political tensions do complicate political relationships, yet somehow our collaborations endure. The Northeast Washington Forest Coalition, for example, has survived unchanged through four presidencies, as our commitment to one another includes buffering the pendulum swings of national politics. But in Donald Trump's first term, his antics made relationships with some WDFW stakeholders difficult. While I lost some friends, I was pleasantly surprised that these tensions did not reduce my ability to call on commitments to support WDFW's biodiversity budget. The agency's budget has grown nicely, and I am hopeful that in the years and decades ahead, not only will biodiversity be better stewarded in the field, but the agency's culture and composition will evolve accordingly. The biggest threat to this optimistic outlook remains the litigious and combative nature of some advocates who sow the whirlwind of culture war. There are activists and groups who agree with the objective of biodiversity but who make it difficult through their hardline positions and tactics with respect to wolf recovery, certain hunting practices, and other agendas seemingly driven by a perspective more focused on the well-being of individual animals than of thriving ecosystems and biodiversity, not to mention democracy.

16

What Brower and Foreman Got Wrong

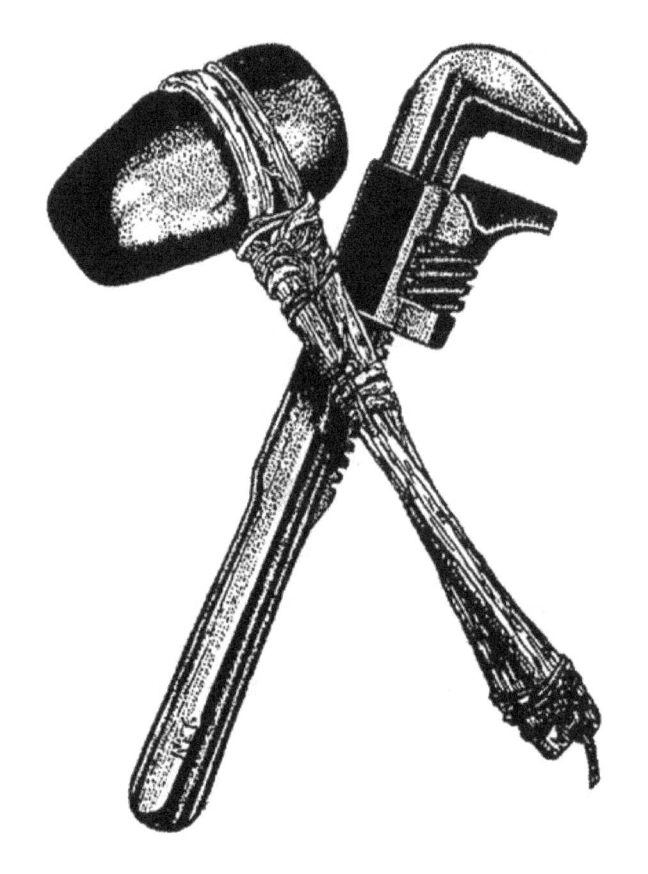

Earth First! logo
(public domain image)

David Brower was arguably the most important conservation leader of the twentieth century. After World War II, where he applied his backcountry and mountaineering skills in the famous 10th Mountain Division's sweep through Italy, he grew the Sierra Club into a national powerhouse. He went on to help found Friends of the Earth, League of Conservation Voters, and Earth Island Institute.

Brower was a compelling speaker, addressing packed audiences at colleges and conferences. He had a personal mission to recruit for the movement and would give time to activists, often in the bar following his speech. His usual drink was Tanqueray and Tonic, "Hold the fruit."

I first met Dave in 1986, when he keynoted an Earth Day celebration I organized at the University of Washington. He helped heal my relationship with my mother and stepfather, when they traveled west to spend a week-long road trip celebrating my college graduation. We got off on the wrong foot when they had to pick me up outside the jail in Benton County, Oregon, where I had just served a week for the billboard debacle. Our road trip took us to the Bay Area and a visit to the Browers' log house in Berkeley for a brunch of his famous strawberry waffles and a reassuring chat. I have nothing but fondness and admiration for David Brower and his legacy.

Brower's boilerplate speech varied little over the years. He had found the words to convey urgency and to inspire a movement to action. Among them was this: "I founded Friends of the Earth to make the Sierra Club look moderate. Dave Foreman founded Earth First! to make Friends of the Earth look moderate. Your job is to make Earth First! look moderate."

Dave Foreman was also a friend to me. Like Brower, he gave great speeches. His charisma in person and in writing elevated him to figurehead status among the cabal of large, bearded men who founded Earth First! in 1980, even though the founder who was more on the frontlines was Mike Roselle. Foreman was more bookish than his public persona let on, considering himself an amateur historian and philosopher. The conservatism of his youth (he campaigned for Barry Goldwater) was stretched and tested but never extinguished, even as the early brashness of Earth First! evolved to accept, foment, and project such nodes as Gandhian civil disobedience, ecofeminism, biocentric deep ecology, conservation biology, and political anarchism. The essence of the movement remained the principle flouted in its tagline: "No compromise in defense of Mother Earth!"

The gambit that both Daves made in pushing boundaries had seeming merit, though its legacy is mixed. The context was the 1980s, two decades after the explosive emergence of environmentalism into American politics with the likes of Rachel Carson and Ralph Nader, then the giant marches of the first Earth Day in 1970. A slate of landmark laws passed in the years following, including the National Environmental Policy Act, Endangered Species Act, and expansion of the Clean Water Act, all signed by President Richard Nixon. Then Jimmy Carter passed the Alaska National Interest Land Conservation Act and put solar panels on the White House roof. In 1981, Ronald Reagan removed those solar panels and filled top positions with avowed anti-environment, anti-regulation evangelists like James Watt and Anne Gorsuch. The logging of national forests almost doubled in the `80s, though some wilderness legislation continued to pass. Special interests were working to break the high and bipartisan public support that the environment still mostly enjoyed. Political momentum was waning, even as scientists elevated warnings about biodiversity and climate.

Dave and Dave responded by calling for boldness. Metaphorically shoot for the moon so you may attain the mountaintop. Ask for a lot, and you might get more than if you had not. These days we refer to this tactic as extending the Overton Window. It has debatable effectiveness, though it surely deserves a page in every strategy handbook. Maybe even the first page. But not the only page!

Brower and Foreman inspired a generation of activists and a blossoming of new organizations and energy. Count me as Exhibit A. My 1988 proposal for bold science-based conservation to protect the Greater North Cascades Ecosystem fits in that "think big" frame, though the ways it paid off for the ecosystem were not as I originally envisioned. Other campaigns that adopted the all-or-nothing approach fared less well. One was the Zero Cut movement.

I have described Clinton's Northwest Forest Plan of 1994 as a big win, protecting way more ancient forest than we might have expected. Many of my peers disagreed. CNW chose to embrace the plan and invested in working within its parameters to maximize its impact, eventually evolving collaborative tactics to focus logging on over-abundant small trees while protecting big ones. Others responded to the Northwest Forest Plan by calling for an end to commercial logging on federal land altogether.

The heart of this End Commercial Logging (ECL), aka Zero Cut, movement was in western Oregon, though it spread widely. Its leaders fomented a rebellion inside the Sierra Club, ousting national board members until they controlled enough votes in 1996 to pass an ECL resolution. Though the movement continued for another couple of decades, that little coup within the Sierra Club board marked its zenith. I do not think they ever had any positive impact on the actual forests. Maybe it was just a polarizing culture war within the conservation movement itself. Another word for such an internal war would be *cancer*. Fortunately, the movement and idea are dead today, though some of its early leaders continue their old habits. Though not all of them. Mike Petersen was once a leader in the ECL movement. He, like me, was active in Washington Earth First! in the 1980s, then spent the 1990s fighting Inland Northwest timber sales by appeal and litigation from his Spokane office. Then he joined with Duane Vaagen and others to found the Northeast Washington Forest Coalition and has spent the last quarter-century collaborating thoughtfully and effectively for better forest management and wildland protection.

I never saw merit in ECL, ecologically, socially, or politically. Just because an idea fits on a bumper sticker does not mean it solves problems in the world. Zero Cut even had a sister campaign, Zero Cud, aiming to eliminate livestock from public land. The net effect of both was to engender more deeply entrenched opposition from the timber and beef industries. I wonder what that energy might have achieved had it been channeled more strategically.

I see such stuff as self-indulgent. Idealists of the sort that back Zero Cut (or marginal political candidates) offer rationalizations like "I have a right to speak my truth" and, when confronted with the likely outcome, "maybe if things get really bad it will wake people up." It never happens. Things get better by getting better, not worse. Momentum builds on winning, not losing. Credibility and support grow through progress and solutions.

Dave Foreman and Earth First! were also notorious for promoting monkeywrenching, property damage intended to stop environmental destruction. Foreman even published a field manual. As mentioned earlier, I dabbled in it myself, doing such things as pulling out survey stakes that would have guided bulldozers pushing roads into wild forest and toppling that billboard. I also once spiked a stand of old-growth forest, which may have been a reason that it still stands. But my role was really to be the guy in the public eye, leading nonviolent civil disobedience protests rather than monkeywrenching.

It is hard to assess the overall effectiveness of monkeywrenching, as incidents were largely kept secret. I tend to think it was mostly bombast. I also tend to think that much of it was poorly targeted. One painful example was damage done to logging equipment just outside of Bellingham. The equipment was owned by a small family business that was cutting second- or third-growth trees in an area of low ecological value on private land near the city and the highway—the very type of place where we should be getting our wood products! How many monkeywrenchers had the knowledge, skill, and courage to do their damage where it would have the greatest impact?

Some people did escalate in a way that, as David Brower urged, made Earth First! look reasonable. I will resist using Ted Kaczynsky, the so-called Unabomber, as an example, as scholars have revealed him to have been more a one-off violent deviant than part of any trendline in the movement. But Earth Liberation Front played with fire around the turn of the millennium. Among their incendiary targets was the University of Washington's much-loved Center for Urban Horticulture, a poplar tree plantation, and a factory processing horse meat. The first two targets were motivated by concern over genetic engineering, with the slight problem that there was no genetic engineering going on in them. As for the third target, I know that people really love horses, but they are also a non-native species, overpopulated feral herds of which do substantial damage to some grasslands in the American West. (While there were North American horses prior to the Pleistocene extinctions, they were relatively small and had different ecology, including that their populations were controlled by abundant but now-absent predators.) If these incidents are any indication, then promoting such tactics might inspire zealots to actions that do more harm than good.

All of this reinforces something I was once told by Hazel Wolf, a Seattle icon and lifelong political organizer and leader in the Northwest who passed away in 2000 at the age of one hundred and two. I once asked Hazel for her for thoughts on aggressive tactics (like tree spiking and monkeywrenching) in light of a sense of desperate urgency to save nature. Hazel replied that she was not a fan. Over the course of her long life, she had seen so many things, many that she herself had worked on, that had gotten so much better. Hazel did not believe shouting "fire" in a theater would be helpful, even if the theater was actually burning.

Perhaps I come across as prudish—an old fogey admonishing young rabble-rousers. Fair enough. But my concerns with monkeywrenching might be more practical than moral. In his novel *The Ministry for the Future*, Kim Stanley Robinson envisions a secretive agency of the United Nations that effectively and aggressively uses the most extreme tactics to finally force a global break with fossil fuels and save the world from climate change. I would welcome that! But from what I have seen, these tools are more likely employed in the wrong ways by the wrong people and on the wrong issues with predictably bad results.

Part IV

Coexistence

17

Hope, Heritage, and Habitat Connections

Lynx released to the southern Kettle Mountains on Colville Indian Reservation in February, 2022
(photo by Michelle Campobasso,
Colville Tribal Fish & Wildlife)

We restructured CNW around our fifteenth anniversary, in 2004, as I mentioned earlier. It was a sensible choice on one hand. We had recently adopted a more collaborative approach to forest work that, in retrospect, might have marked an end for us of the long ancient forest war. We were also five years beyond our Loomis Forest success. On the other hand, we were still deep in the massive campaign to protect habitat linking the North and South Cascades across the ecological fracture zone of I-90 around Snoqualmie Pass. Also, the country was in a somber mood from both a recession and President George W. Bush's ill-fated invasion of Iraq. Yet we decided to start preparing for our next big thing.

One other factor contributed to our thinking. A team of scientists led by Peter Singleton modeled habitat connectivity for the region's montane wildlife that still guides our landscape conservation work today.

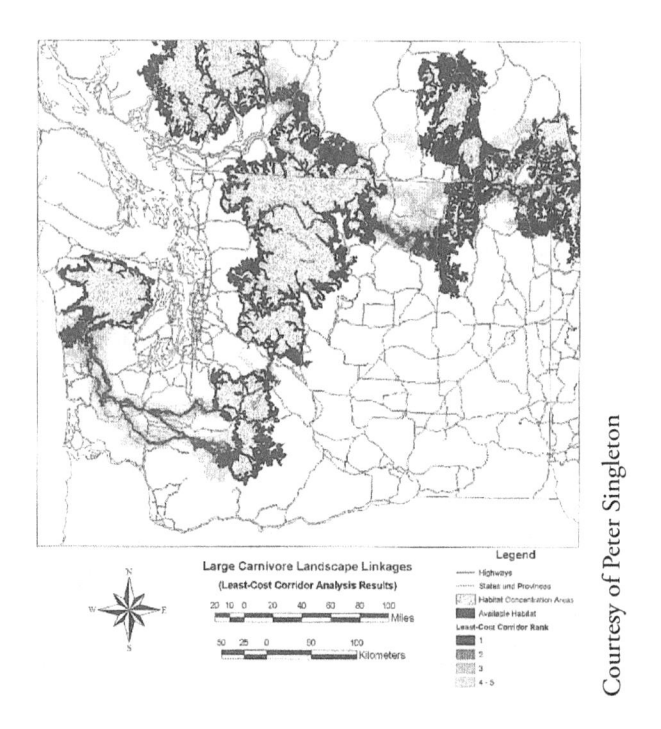

Large Carnivore Landscape Linkages
(Least-Cost Corridor Analysis Results)

Courtesy of Peter Singleton

Our strategic restructuring included a merger with a group in northeast Washington and taking on its staff to expand our efforts there to protect the habitat corridor linking wildlife populations from the North Cascades to the Rockies. Renamed as Conservation Northwest, we hoped our new brand would better enable us to build a big tent for conservation. And finally, we adopted the public messaging posture of "hope and heritage."

Hope contrasts with the alienating doom-and-gloom messaging of many environmentalists. This was a deliberate choice, but not for Pollyannish reasons. I prefer the model of how Winston Churchill led the United Kingdom through its darkest hour—naked truth about dire circumstances coupled with a spirit to overcome. People need hope to come together for tough work. But they are more likely to be hopeful when they feel they are not being deceived.

Heritage for me is a proxy for what we hold in common. I believe love for wild nature is at the heart of the American psyche and experience. This contrasts with how many progressives and environmentalists choose to identify as countercultural. There is substance to my view. True, biocentric values are clearly distinct from those of religious dominion, the pioneering mindset of manifest destiny, or the growth appetite of the industrial era. But why the hell would we choose to antagonize people who still care about clean air and water and who love wildlife? Even those who make money from logging of big trees may have admiration for primeval forests. Even those who fear grizzly bears or despise wolves may have respect and admiration for their power and beauty, perhaps even their ecological functions.

In 2004, we adopted the theme of hope and heritage to implement those strategic fundamentals. It has served us well. Other groups project similar culture and use similar messaging, contributing to big tent coalitions and strategies. The National Wildlife Federation exemplifies it on a national scale, and many of its state affiliates do locally. This is one reason why, in 2016, CNW decided to become the Washington affiliate of NWF.

We also adopted a heightened focus on habitat corridors linking the large ecosystems of our region. At CNW, we think of the North Cascades Ecosystem as a hub in the Northwest regional landscape. Our job is to protect enough of the wild areas and rare habitats within the core ecosystems like the North Cascades to support self-sustaining populations of native wildlife. But some species demand so much space for population viability that even an area as large as the North Cascades Ecosystem will not suffice. We therefore protect corridors that ecologically link the North Cascades south across I-90 to the South Cascades and on to the

Chehalis Basin and Olympic Mountains to the west. Corridors connect the Kettle River Range to the east and on northeasterly to the Canadian Rockies, as well as northwesterly to the Coast and Chilcotin Ranges of British Columbia. We need each of these mountain ecosystems sufficiently protected and interconnected by habitat corridors, including the means to safely cross under or over major roadways that cut across a corridor. The corridors don't just improve the viability of wide-ranging species like wolverines and grizzly bears; they are the first best step for enabling these ecosystems and the species that comprise them to adapt to the changes that global warming is imposing. *Landscape conservation* is the term that describes that whole body or network of habitat protection.

Landscape conservation does not mean protecting the entirety of any landscape. It does mean protecting those parts that enable ecosystems to function, sustain their native species, withstand disturbances (fire, storms), and be resilient and adaptive to the changing climate. In short, protect enough of each kind of habitat in a pattern that allows the whole to persist. Corridors that link together larger areas of protected habitat, like bridges linking islands, are integral to that approach.

Today, many scientists and conservation groups focus on landscape conservation. It is easier to envision and practice in places where there is substantial public land, which tends to be in the mountains and deserts that Teddy Roosevelt took office in time to secure from the ravages of America's industrial robber barons. Every corridor is different, requiring unique means to protect it from unique challenges.

The connections between the North and South Cascades are best represented by the Pacific fisher. Fishers require the old forest habitat that we protected through the Northwest Forest Plan in 1994 and The Cascades Conservation Partnership, from

2001 to 2005. The fishers that we reintroduced into the North and South Cascades are actively using that protected core habitat and those habitat corridors, including highway crossings. It's all one big happy population in one giant and connected ecosystem. Our work continues to increase the permeability of this area for wildlife in ways that improve forest and stream habitats while providing wood and jobs.

CNW's Jen Watkins, Jen Syrowitz (who stepped into Watkins' job when she moved on), and Laurel Baum have taken westside forest restoration to the landscape level. They also engage collaboratively using private funding to actively restore wetlands damaged by unlawful motorized recreation, rehabilitate culvert-choked creeks, and remove unneeded and landslide-prone roads. Laurel and her volunteers even upgraded an antiquated structure at Milepost 27 of I-90 to enable elk to cross through.

Grizzly bears represent the connections from the North Cascades to the Coast and Chilcotin Ranges of British Columbia. We have promoted restoration of grizzlies in the North Cascades since CNW's founding in 1989. It has eluded and confounded us, as we have watched reports of bear sightings dwindle over the years, indicating the small population that existed in the early 1990s has by now all but died out as politics thwarted several pushes for recovery effort. Success may finally be at hand, as the federal government decided in June of 2024 on a plan to move a few grizzlies per year into the North Cascades until at least twenty-five bears are present. The Syilx (or Okanagan) First Nation is also planning to transplant bears into the Canadian side of the ecosystem.

Meanwhile, there is a great need to recover the health of other diminished grizzly bear populations in southwest B.C., lying between the North Cascades and the abundant bear populations of the Chilcotin region. This has been the focus of the Coast to

Cascades Grizzly Bear Initiative, a collaboration between CNW and several First Nations that closely identify with grizzly bears in their cultures. Joe Scott facilitates this effort, which he initiated in 2008. It is beautiful to see bear presence and conservation efforts increase in places such as B.C.'s Pemberton Valley. Coexistence measures like electric fences allow farmers to enjoy the sight of bears without fear for their crops. The St'át'imc First Nation and others are applying their rights and title to protect bear habitat from roads and other threats. Communities like Pemberton and Whistler actively support recovery of grizzlies in their midst, in stark contrast to some North Cascades communities that have been so long without bears that the vacuum of experience has filled with sensationalized fears.

Gray wolves are the best totem for the Cascades to Olympics habitat linkage. The CNW staff met for a scheduled annual planning retreat on Wednesday, November 9, 2016, the day after Donald Trump first won election. The meeting opened with crying, venting, and head-scratching. What happened to our country?

We were at the tail-end of a strategic planning process that had started a year earlier. But those previous months of planning had never considered that Trump would head the government. Was our program still relevant? My first inclination was to revisit all our plans and consider shifting resources to defense. Then it came to mind that Trump's election was a symptom of American polarization, particularly between rural and urban values. We were proud of our work engaging collaboratively in affected communities to find common ground for solutions like forest restoration, wildlife highway crossings, and wolf coexistence. It occurred to us that America needed more of this type of work, not less. And that while fixing America's problems was far beyond our reach, we could and should do at least our part. The outcome of that retreat was a decision to stay the course on all our programs and to launch two entirely new ones: Cascades to Olympics and Sagelands Heritage.

While both the Cascades and Olympic ecosystems are truly wild, they are separated not just by the vast and privately owned industrial timberlands and farm country of the Chehalis Basin but also by Interstate 5, which presents a veritable wall to wildlife, running as it does north-south from Olympia to Vancouver, WA, and the east-west State Route 8/US 12. Tackling this area was an act of courage and optimism, as much of it sits in deeply conservative terrain. I was a holdout, pressing my staff for clarity on what species would be our focus, what conditions we had to work with, and what our prospects were for success. Now, after just a few years of work, we are much farther along than I had dared dream.

CNW's Brian Stewart, a punk-rocking habitat connectivity evangelist, and his volunteers have already cleared a way for elk and other wildlife to cross Route 12 under the bridge that spans the Satsop River. Most remarkably, we are now confident that crossings will be installed where the last two remaining possible habitat corridors intersect I-5. These corridors are of relatively intact remaining habitat extending continuously from around Mt. Rainier and Mt. Adams, respectively, west to the Chehalis Valley. We are working with the Washington Department of Transportation toward locating, designing and finding funding to build appropriate crossings. Our goal is for that to happen by 2030. Meanwhile, we are working with local partners, including the Chehalis Tribe, a land trust, and a couple timber companies, acquiring easements or fee simple ownership to keep the private properties along those two corridors in compatible land uses.

The best wolf habitat in the state is in its southwest corner, where there are fewer people and livestock. Once wolves can cross the interstate, they will easily make it to there and then on up to the Olympics.

Sharp-tailed grouse best represents the sage steppe of eastern Washington. The objective of our Sagelands Heritage Program is to connect arid grassland habitat and species from Washington's Columbia Basin to the Canadian Okanagan region. Jay Kehne and his team are collaborating with farmers, conservation districts, WDFW, the Colville and Yakama Tribes, and others to sustain connected patches of sage steppe habitat among extensive cultivated crops and pastures of this busy landscape. The most exciting new opportunity is the technology of virtual fencing, which I described in the "Better Beef" chapter. The most troubling new threat is alternative energy.

One might expect conservations to eagerly embrace alternative energy. We do. We need it to save ecosystems and civilization from what fossil fuels do to our climate. But utility-scale wind and solar developments can impact vast areas of habitat. Put a solar farm in a narrow connection between two patches of healthy sage steppe and its resident populations of grouse, badger, or pygmy rabbit, and the corridor is gone. Alternative energy can also impact Indian cultural sites and prime farmland. My Sagelands Heritage staff was caught off-guard by this new threat to our objectives, and they have spent countless hours fighting proposed installations in high-conflict places like the south end of Badger Mountain, northeast of Wenatchee.

Fortunately, we have ways of determining what places are best-suited for solar and wind energy production while least conflicting with habitat, culture, and agriculture. Washington State University undertook a process of expert working groups and mapping to identify about a million-and-a-half acres of eastern Washington that are suitable for wind and solar production at least conflict with other landscape values. That is about eight times the acreage needed to meet the state's climate-related alternative energy goal for the year 2050. With effective state leadership and policy, we can meet our energy and climate goals without undermining landscape conservation.

Lynx is the totem for habitat linking the North Cascades to the Rockies, or at least for about half of the great distance this corridor spans. It is best to see this corridor as four distinct segments, each requiring its own approach. The westernmost segment is the most challenging, as it crosses the private lands of the Okanogan River Valley and U.S. Route 97, which has the dubious distinction of the highest rate of wildlife road kills in Washington. I detail our work to remedy that western segment of the corridor in the next chapter.

The second segment is the crest of the Kettle River Range, comprised mostly of roadless national forest running north from the Colville Indian Reservation to the Canadian border. Then on the British Columbia side of the Kettles, where Joe and partners, led by the Okanagan (Syilx) First Nation, are laying groundwork for conserving key grizzly bear habitat that we believe will sustain the function of that stretch of the linkage. Last is the northeast segment, which is the West Kootenay region of southeast B.C. That area includes parts of the five and a half million acres that the province protected in its 2008 Mountain Caribou Recovery Plan, an outcome from a five-year campaign called the Mountain Caribou Project that we conducted with a regional partner, Wildsight. In late 2023, the B.C. government announced an ambitious conservation finance policy, backed by over a billion dollars, to protect priority ancient forests across the province. That policy hopefully will fill important gaps in the conservation needs of the Kootenay region.

Gaining permanent protection for the roadless crest of the Kettle Range is critical for this overall linkage, which is so long that we see it less as a single corridor than as one or more steppingstones—the Kettle Range being the most important—linked by corridors. CNW has worked since 2004 to secure permanent protection for the wildlands of the Kettle Crest. Our original belief was that collaborating with timber and community interests would have great political currency. For two decades, the timber and conservation sides have held up our respective ends. We accomplished much for the forests and communities, restoring thousands of acres of forest through active management that provided jobs and incomes. But we fell short of the clout needed to even get a bill introduced into Congress to protect the Kettle Crest. We continue the effort by encouraging the leadership of the Colville Tribes to pursue a tribal-led national monument that would simultaneously benefit wildlife, salmon, and cultural heritage.

Meanwhile, in a gratifying partnership with the Colville and other Tribes and First Nations, we have succeeded in reintroducing lynx to the Kettle Range. With Dave Werntz as our lead, we have over the past four years trapped thirty-six lynxes in the mountains east of Kelowna, B.C. and released them in the southern Kettle Mountains on the Colville Indian Reservation. We plan for one more year of effort, aiming for fifty cats. I have had the thrill of being present both at the trapping of a lynx and for the release of another. Each involved an "I'm not worthy" feeling to experience the calm and serenity, not to mention the beauty, of being so near such a cool cat. When I witnessed the release of a lynx into the mountain forests of the southern Kettle Mountains in November of 2021, it was thirty-three years after my initial efforts to protect this species and its habitat. I had protested logging of their habitat, successfully petitioned the federal government to protect them under the Endangered Species Act, and raised vast sums to ransom their Loomis Forest habitat. I had surely paid my dues to have that moment. But looking into her eyes, which projected neither acceptance nor rejection but more graceful neutrality, my sense was of being an interloper.

CNW advances other programs besides protecting corridors and restoring carnivores. A staff of four works to restore forests and watersheds on federal land. We have a Wildlife and Recreation Coexistence team, led by rock jock Kurt Hellman, that seeks ways to protect wildlife and the treaty rights of Tribal partners, mostly the Tulalip and Snoqualmie, from the ever-growing hordes of people who cherish the Cascades for hiking, biking, and other recreational pursuits, often unaware of their impacts or how to minimize them. Alishia Orloff leads our work with eastern Washington Tribes on the protection and perpetuation of Tribal first foods, including through fostering cultural burning. The plants and animals that have deep value to Indians as traditional foods and medicines also serve as proxies for healthy wildlife habitat. Conserving one serves the other. As I noted earlier, Similkameen Chief Rob Edward says, "If there isn't food for the grizzly, there isn't food for me."

The composite of all this landscape conservation work is a regionally connected network of habitat that sustains wildlife, is adaptive to climate change, improves human lives, and does not increase regulatory burdens. We have accomplished all this while seeing (and in cases causing) the return into former range wildlife including fishers, wolves, wolverines, lynxes, and soon grizzly bears. We have made all this progress not only without resorting to polarizing tactics, but while in degrees building community support and mutual understanding. Our work is not easy or panacea. We still face plenty of opposition and recalcitrant attitudes that are hostile to conservation. Change does not please everyone. But in large measure, we are doing our part to fix America, both ecologically and socially.

18

From Polarization to Progress in Okanogan County

Colville children at Figlenski Ranch event
(photo Jasmine Minbashian)

Conserving the western segment of the Cascades to Rockies corridor, where it crosses the Okanogan River Valley, is a continuing effort of over fifteen years, monumental in both its challenge and success. This is the heart of deeply conservative Okanogan County. When we started work to protect this stretch of the habitat corridor in 2007, we faced local resentment rooted in memories of my radical past. But the goal of sustaining this landscape objective attracted allies. We formed yet another coalition, called the Working for Wildlife Initiative. Our immediate challenge was that a key property was being marketed for residential development that would have blocked the last best place for wildlife to traverse part of U.S. Route 97, extinguishing much of the functional connection between the Cascades and the Kettle and Rocky Mountain Ranges.

With partners including WDFW, Okanogan Land Trust, and Trust for Public Lands, we accessed state and federal funds to acquire that particular property, which became the state's 2,240-acre Carter Mountain Wildlife Area. We have since protected a half-dozen other properties totaling over twenty thousand acres through a variety of means. Each continues in management compatible with wildlife use and traverse, including by lynx. Some properties remain held by ranchers but with conservation easements. One we purchased as CNW, put an easement on it, then resold it encumbered to conservation-focused owners.

The best stories here are of how we overcame great challenges through collaboration to establish wildlife crossings on Route 97 and acquire the Figlenski Ranch for the Colville Tribes. These stories tell of how land and community can heal together.

"That makes sense. But if CNW is for it, then I'm against it."

That is what Jim Detro, an Okanogan County Commissioner, said when CNW's Jay Kehne proposed that we get underpasses built through the highway to make it safer for both wildlife and drivers. Detro is an old conservative warhorse in a county full of them. He remembers the forest wars and has a low opinion of me. He once said about me to *The Seattle Times*: "Once an egg-sucking dog, always an egg-sucking dog." (For the record, I have never sucked an egg.) Jay overcame Detro's opposition by pulling together some of his hunting buddies to form a local chapter of the Mule Deer Foundation. That group then spearheaded the effort to build local support for underpasses. Everyone was already familiar with the hazard that crossing deer posed to drivers, so Jay's gang needed only to show that the solution was benign. One rancher whose property abutted the highway was concerned that the fencing associated with the crossings would impair his access. Jay addressed his concerns and won his support. To help the state legislature see this as a priority, we raised a quarter-million dollars in private donations, which we spent on fencing a mile on each side of a key stretch of the highway. We also used volunteers to clear brush and trash from under a bridge spanning the Okanogan River. Those simple measures reduced deer collisions in that stretch by over ninety percent, and WSDOT's automated cameras have recorded thousands of animals, from deer to turkeys, now passing under that bridge.

This common-sense project unified the local voice, including the Okanogan County Commission. That enabled us to persuade the state legislature to commit over $3.7 million to the objective. Our focus now is to leverage those state funds into a big federal grant for the construction of formal underpasses. I expect that soon there will be at least three ways for wildlife to cross under the highway in the critical twelve-mile stretch where it intersects the Cascades to Rockies habitat corridor.

I mentioned the Figlenski Ranch earlier, in the "Better Beef" chapter, which opened with Jay Kehne and I hunting for deer on this property. The ranch sits east of Route 97, in the Tunk Creek Valley, a few miles north of the Colville Indian Reservation's northern border. That reservation is huge, with 1.4 million acres. But it was originally double that size—extending all the way to the Canadian border when established in 1872. The federal government reduced it to its present size in 1892, primarily to allow settlers to mine gold. The people of the Colville, a confederation of twelve different Tribes sharing this reservation, still refer to that area as the "North Half."

The Figlenski family came from Wisconsin in 1904 to homestead on the North Half. Their ranch grew over four generations to be larger than seventeen thousand acres, comprising the most important private property in the Cascades to Rockies habitat corridor. When I became aware of the property about fifteen years ago, there were four members of the family—the aged third-generation couple and their two bachelor sons, Ernie and Eddy, both in their sixties. By 2020, only Ernie Figlenski remained, and the ranch was at risk of being broken up for housing. I had failed for years to find a conservation buyer for the ranch. Purchase by a public agency would not have been politically feasible. I wondered if ownership by the Colville Tribes would work.

I knew from his neighbors that Ernie cared a great deal for the land, its wildlife, and the family's heritage. I inquired through his lawyer whether he was open to tribal ownership and was delighted to learn that he was. But Ernie wanted assurance that the Tribes would maintain the property as open space for agriculture and wildlife. That was a problem, as I knew that the Colville Tribal Business Council would view a conservation easement as infringing on their sovereignty. I proposed to tribal leadership that they adopt by council resolution certain covenants that had been drafted by our expert land use attorney, Konrad Liegel (his actual name!). In binding themselves by these covenants, the Tribes would be making a reasonable commitment to conservation without relinquishing their sovereignty to any outside entity. With excellent work by the Tribes' then natural resources director, Cody Desautel, the Council accepted the concept. Ernie and I proceeded to sign an option agreement on February 1, 2021, giving CNW six months to raise enough funds to purchase 9,740 acres. The balance of the acreage had already been sold, mostly to the neighboring ranch run by friends Jim and Nancy Soriano, but also five hundred acres to a developer.

Three weeks later, I drove to the reservation to watch the Colville Tribal Business Council pass its resolution approving the covenants. A brutal storm made the drive treacherous, closing Stevens Pass (U.S. Highway 2) during my morning drive east and Snoqualmie Pass (Interstate 90) during my afternoon return. The temperatures were well below zero in the Okanogan Valley. When I got home that evening, I was ready to celebrate the Council's action, not to mention surviving the journey. Then I got a call from Jim Soriano; Ernie had died that morning while feeding his cattle in the bitter cold.

Over the following half-year, we raised the four-and-a-half million dollars needed for the purchase. The Nature Conservancy helped by contributing funds that Eddy Figlenski had left for them in his will several years before. We wired the funds into escrow, and the deed (with covenants attached) passed directly to the Colville Tribes. This is the largest privately funded Land

Back (i.e. return of land to Tribes) action in the history of the American West.

The Tribes hosted a ceremony on the property that October. Standing together for speeches in the fall rain were Indian elders, ranching neighbors (including Figlenski relatives), local elected leaders, and conservation donors. I choked up during my speech, recalling the challenges and Ernie's passing. Whatever reputations or old resentments had been or still were in any minds, on this day we stood together to honor the heritage of the Tribes, a pioneer family, and the land and wildlife that is firmament, common ground to us all. It is a place that lynx will at times traverse as they move between their populations around the Loomis Forest in the Cascades and now in the Kettle Range. We did all of that, and I can hardly believe it.

19

Conservation, Citizenship, and Democracy

Author lobbying in D.C., March 2018
(photo by the author)

When I was a young, hotheaded Earth First!er, I was not thinking too far ahead. My view was that industrial humanity was a scourge on the wild Earth, and that only immediate radical action would save nature, if not also humanity. The Deep Ecology revolution never happened, yet we and our planet remain, albeit with declining biodiversity and a climate that is changing with perilous speed. Adding to our troubles, illiberalism has risen in America and abroad. If I once took for granted the democracy within which I pursued my conservation goals, that innocence is gone. This shift started thirty years ago, when I toured Siberia.

"It is not safe for you here anymore. You will have to leave," said Ivan.

He was the leader of the street gang that was hosting me and my friend Dana Lyons, along with our translator/guide, Eric Sievers, in a rundown apartment in Vladivostok, on Russia's southeastern coast. Their gang was an unusual one: veterans of the Russian Navy who shared interest in Buddhism and environmental conservation. You read correctly—a Russian street gang of Buddhist environmentalists!

One of their members had just entered the apartment with a bloodied face, having been jumped by rivals. With a gang war at hand, Dana and I were put on a train to a nature preserve now called Land of the Leopard National Park, about an hour west of the city.

This was July of 1993. We were on a three-week tour of eastern Russia as activist tourists. Weyerhaeuser Lumber Company was trying to gain rights to log in the giant wilderness around the Botcha River in the Sikhote-Alin region of the Far East. A year before, I had met Valari Zograf in Everett, Washington. Valari was a humble schoolteacher and naturalist who led the charge against Weyerhaeuser from his home in the city of Sovetskaya Gavan. Weyerhaeuser had arranged for him to visit Washington to educate him about forestry, which didn't work out as they had hoped. My meeting with Valari prompted this adventure, which began with us first attending a conference about forests in Lesosibirsk, a part of central Siberia that Russia had only recently opened to Westerners. Then we rode the Trans-Siberian Railroad three thousand miles to the Far East. It was a rich experience with culture and nature. Relevant here is what I learned about politics in that crumbling society.

The optimistic period of President Gorbachev's Perestroika had already ended, but the beginning of Putin's despotic reign was still a few years off. Nobody knew what Russia's future would be. We witnessed the ghostly legacies of failed Communism, and the fits-and-starts attempts at capitalism and democracy. Mostly, we witnessed dysfunction and decay of civilization. The elevators in the dreary Soviet block-style apartment buildings were typically broken, and stairwells smelled like urine. At times, failed plumbing required us to flush toilets with buckets of water.

I remember sitting in Valari's apartment in Sov Gavan. His TV set happened to be on, and it showed a psychic with mystical plates spinning behind her.

Valari rolled his eyes and lamented the brain drain they suffer in the Far East. "Since Stalin, intelligent people have moved to either Moscow or gulags."

I don't want to mislead you. It was an amazing journey with incredible high points, including time with dedicated conservation activists and scientists. We also flew in a giant helicopter deep into the Botcha wilderness, where we found the skull of a brown bear and I fished big trout from the wild river.

During our closing days of the trip, after being shuttled away from the gang war, we were in Kedrovaya Pad Zapovednik, a reserve within Land of the Leopard National Park. An American biologist named Dick allowed us to tag along as he tracked radio signals from an Amur leopard he had collared. I asked him if Siberian tigers still roamed this area.

"No," he replied. "Their shrunken range peters out hundreds of miles to the north. But if they were here, this tree (an oak leaning out over the trail) is the sort that a tiger would use to mark its territory."

I noticed something orange wedged in the tree's bark and pulled out what was clearly a clump of tiger hair. Dick's face reacted in surprise, and a tingling rose along the back of my neck.

Nonetheless, our final experiences drove home my conclusion about Russia's dark side. Dana and I flew home from Vladivostok on separate days. On the day of my flight, we were back in the apartment of that Buddhist gang and had lost track of time. Ivan summoned a taxi and menacingly instructed the driver to get me to my flight, or else. The poor guy was sweating even before we hit a big traffic jam. Unbelievably, he drove us on the shoulder of the opposing traffic lanes to get us around the backup. It was madness! When we reached the accident that was the cause of the backup, I noticed it involved a car that had veered off the highway and rammed into a utility pole. I recall the vehicle having been sheared in two, and at least one body on the roadway. Policemen were poking at the body, playfully, laughing. My taxi driver crossed himself, which I found strangely reassuring.

Back in Bellingham, Dana told me of his airport ordeal. While he was waiting in the terminal, a gang of conspicuous thugs entered the area and made themselves comfortable. A flight landed, and passengers disembarked. When the guy they were waiting for came through the door, the thugs beat the shit out of him right there in the terminal. For a deep view of the Soviet and post-Soviet world, check out *Patriot*, the recent posthumous autobiography of Alexei Navalny, the Russian opposition leader who was killed in 2024.

I had gone to Russia an idealist, well-read in the likes of Howard Zinn and Noam Chomsky, attuned to America's shortcomings. I returned home counting my blessings as an American. My hopes that Russia would trend upward did not pan out. But I sure did not expect autocracy to resurge there and elsewhere, as it has. Even less did I expect to see it to infect the United States.

I do believe that conservationists have a role in helping cool the fever, or at least not further inflaming it. We are all stewards of the accumulated capital of a healthy, liberal, democratic, and hopefully prosperous society. Conservationists deplete that capital at great peril to our democracy, and in turn, nature.

When conservationists stoke polarization, it runs counter to the broader objectives of civil society. Like an evil djinn in a bottle, polarization carries alluring power but at high cost. Brandishing strong words about the sacred (e.g. wolves) and the profane (wolf killers in agriculture or government) can win riches of media coverage, donations, and legislative leverage. Its incendiary power is that it draws on our tribal tendencies to distinguish "others" from ourselves. At one pole are the good guys (our side), while at the other are the evil ones (tree cutters, wolf killers, rednecks). Demonization stirs great passion among supporters but shrinks common ground and kills prospects for negotiation.

People naturally dislike being the object of demonization and long remember it.

This behavior is a favor to the political right. Conservative idealogues aspire to have government so small that private industry can operate unfettered. As Grover Norquist famously said, "I don't want to abolish government. I simply want to reduce it to the size where I can drag it into the bathroom and drown it in the bathtub." Organizations that exist to complain and sue while using the strongest rhetoric in media and fundraising appeals are winning Pyrrhic victories. Public faith in our institutions is historically weak; people today are cynical about government. That cynicism is tinder for demagogues to exploit.

Trump campaigned in 2016 promising to "drain the swamp," meaning he would neutralize the lobbyists and powerful interests that keep government from giving his voters whatever outcomes they yearn for. Instead, he put those lobbyists and special interests at his side, where they worked to neutralize our government's ability to serve the broader public interest. One example is how he shifted the headquarters and core staff of the Bureau of Land Management from Washington, D.C. to distant Colorado, so it would be ineffective in protecting our resources from the petroleum interests that gained a powerful advantage. He also shifted the balance of the U.S. Supreme Court to a majority that favors business over the public and its government. In 2024, the Court ruled on a key case, nicknamed Chevron, in such a way that undermines judicial deference to government agencies and experts. This is likely to sweep away those regulations (protecting land, air, water, and life) that are not directly stated in statutes passed by Congress. Special interests will feast on this weakening of our laws and agencies, while our Congress remains divided and hapless.

If we want our government to be effective in protecting and restoring nature, we citizens need a relationship with it that can enable success. That means more than shouting at or suing agencies for their shortcomings.

Our role as both citizens and nature advocates is not only to make demands of government, but to help it succeed in efficiently meeting the interests that we and other stakeholders have in common. Daniel Kemmis's book, *Community and the Politics of Place*, argues that citizenship includes finding solutions at the community level which government can then enact. He presents how this was an original vision and practice of the founders. This is in stark contrast to the model that many now hold, in which government exists to respond between competing shrill interests and that policy outcomes should be based on which side generates the most activist emails. Not that there is anything wrong with activist emails; I just wish we could wield them in greater service of the big picture.

When a collaborative group that involves bona fide diverse interests (conservation, timber, recreation, community) finds common ground on the use of science-based forest practices and protections for local public lands, their government (the Forest Service, Congress) ought to give due weight to that agreement. Collaborative outcomes can be more durable while also lubricating the gears of democracy. In contrast, when activists appeal immediately to political or judicial power, it can act like sand in those gears. The latter may feel like a more direct path to an objective, but is it really?

This does not mean that those who live closest to a public resource should control it. Public resources belong to the public and often are of national interest. But locals have a valid stake and often valuable knowledge, and we should hear their voice. The owners of a local sawmill or ranch may have human interests beyond their business motives. I have found people like Maurice Williamson, the Vaagens (Duane's engagement has been succeeded by that of his sons, Russ and then Kurtis), John Squires, the Gothams and Dawsons, and other rural resource-dependent people to care deeply about their communities and about nature. Engaging with them in a fair process is just and has the prospect of outcomes that meet the interests and objectives of all stakeholders, including nature.

Collaboration will not always work, but it is always worth a try. As Churchill said, "Meeting jaw to jaw is better than war." From my experience, I also see truth in the axiom that it's easier to start a war than to end one. Yet conservationists often resort first to conflict without even trying to know the other people and perspectives involved. Our democracy offers and requires so much more than that.

One might ask whether conservation really causes resentment of the depth I describe. While the top issues that fuel America's polarized culture wars include abortion, race, gender, and guns, climate change registers as well. According to Pew polling, about 80 percent of Democrats see "global climate change as a major threat to the country" while only about 25 percent of Republicans do. Issues like wolf recovery, forest management, water policy, and farmland regulation also register, at least on local scales. The red and blue of a political map separate cleanly along the urban/rural divide. Rural newspapers in my state often cover wildlife and land issues, commonly with invective. Legislators who represent rural districts often hype these same issues in their constituent communications. If newspapers and politicians function as though wildlife and land issues stoke passion, we should believe them.

In Washington, we have achieved wolf recovery in a way that not only involves less wolf mortality than in any other state, but also fosters bipartisan collaboration in Olympia to advance and fund effective policy. That has been good for both the wolves and Washington. Not only do we not have to waste effort in unproductive legislative posturing, but there are fewer resentful ranchers or hunters motivated to "make liberals cry" by poaching a wolf.

I do not see this as a concession or compromise to appease an adversary. We need healthy rural communities and should want to help them. They grow our food and manage our forests, and they face huge economic headwinds. Technology allows farms and forests to operate with a fraction of the labor it took fifty years ago, which means many schools and downtowns are empty, while many others are full of recent urban escapees who drive up the cost of housing and the development value of farm ground. Media on the left and right run on a business model that finds purchase in stoking resentment between urban and rural America. It is harmful to all of us, but to conservationists perhaps above all. The nature we care about is not among the skyscrapers where most of us and our supporters live. Our job should be to bridge the urban/rural divide, not to inflame or exploit it.

I see none of this in writings on environmental strategy. Such books give advice on using Saul Alinsky tactics to build and flex political power. Those tactics are invaluable at times and were key in saving ancient forests. But tactics of mass political mobilization are better-suited to social issues (sometimes including environmental justice) than protection of wild nature. The political pressure from big rallies and letter-writing campaigns falls on urban politicians, not the ones with wolves, ancient forests, and wildlands in their districts. Urban politicians may genuinely care for nature, and some serve as legislative champions. But most Democrats and their floor leaders logically prioritize issues that are more visceral to their urban constituents. Meanwhile, those rural newspapers are full of articles about wolves, cougars, and wildfires, giving leverage to the conservative

Republicans who represent those communities in legislative bodies.

Indirect approaches like collaboration are not passive. If one tries to negotiate without power, nature will lose. You gain hard power by having the means to resort to litigation or legislation if collaboration fails. Also available is the soft power of broad coalitions (with Tribes, hunters/anglers, hikers, birdwatchers), persuasive arguments based in science and economics, and shared values. I think of power as being like a ratchetting socket wrench. The handle represents influences (coalitions, collaborations, protests, litigation) that provide leverage for movement. But we lock in the gains from that movement with the ratchet, which represents negotiated or legislated outcomes that are durable.

Advocacy movements are themselves a curious ecosystem. When I got my start in the mid-1980s, there were not a lot of Washingtonians making a living fighting for nature. Now it's hard to walk around Olympia or D.C. without tripping over lobbying colleagues. From the outside perspective of, say, a disinterested logging or ranching family, the group names and acronyms must seem way beyond comprehension. They assume we are coordinated and perhaps even interchangeable. I wish it were so. The vast array of issues—from climate to toxics to oceans to urban growth to the wildland issues I work on—does justify a corresponding bevy of groups with specialized focus. But within the space of land and wildlife conservation, the distribution is confounding. On issues like wolves and national forests, the funder and activist concentration are high enough that it can be a scrum of counterproductivity, like all the passengers on a boat scurrying to one side and causing it to list. New activists and groups join the dogpile without due consideration of whether they add value. Andy Kerr once told me that he aspired to write a book about the forest protection movement, which he would title, *In Spite of Ourselves*. In the business world, if companies compete, the market will tend to deliver results that are measurable and foster accountability. Supposedly, that has something to do with Adam Smith's invisible hand. Too bad the guy did not put his other hand to use directing deference and efficiency among the efforts of nonprofit groups!

When advocates reach our objectives without creating or perpetuating adversaries, we build honor and momentum. If we open a respectful conversation, genuinely listening to concerns and interests as well as expressing our own, we may succeed in aiding nature, community, and democracy. Paradoxically, we may be more likely to win if we fight less aggressively, as other stakeholders are less adversarial when we are not shouting in their faces. And if we can peacefully resolve issues like how best to manage our forests, streams, and wildlife, we may reduce the culture war resistance to solving the harder and existential issue of climate change.

We conservationists must care about the larger issues of our democracy, even if only because an effective and rational government is more likely to advance good environmental policy. We therefore have good reason to pursue conservation goals through means that are least likely to agitate rural voters, contribute to toxic polarization, and prepare the ground for autocracy.

20

Advocacy: Doing Something Is Better Than Being Something

Habitat restoration work party near I-90 Rocky Run
Wildlife Undercrossing, Oct. 2015
(photo by Alaina Kowitz,
courtesy of Conservation Northwest)

There is a temptation within us to want to be something, to have a validating identity to which we can cling. I am an American, a Jew, a Husky, a Seahawk fan. I am a conservationist. Evolution hardwired us this way for good reason, as intratribal bonds and aversion to "others" (who might carry bad intentions or infectious diseases) imbued fitness in the ancient world. But like our appendix, tonsils, wisdom teeth, and taste for simple sugars, our ancient fitness is today maladaptive.

Identities can be meaningful if based on principles worth representing and at times defending, like the U.S. Constitution. Others are less so. The writer Kurt Vonnegut referred to such identities as granfalloons, "a proud and meaningless collection of human beings." Meaningless does not always mean harmless.

Contemporary culture is obsessed with performative identity. This may come from the ideological sorting of social media algorithms, or the mobility offered by today's workplaces and communities. We live, work, and play within bubbles of the like-minded and perform to them for acceptance. A result is what has come to be called *wokeness*, by which standards for behavior are set and enforced by the cultural crowd. The sociologist Musa al-Gharbi published his book *We Have Never Been Woke* in 2024. He presents a history of the term "woke," its appearance in previous cycles of American culture and politics as far back as the post-Civil War era, the circumstances that seem to foster it, and its consequences. None of it is encouraging. He ascribes its motives as performative among privileged classes and its results as accruing no actual benefit to lower classes. Results include resentment and alienation. Polling shows that the vast majority of the Latino community objects strenuously to the term Latinx. Similarly, most of the Black community is not on board with defunding the police, a call which swept through progressive politics after the killing of George Floyd. Similar sentiments have been measured for the culturally enforced use of pronouns. Al-Gharbi argued in his online Substack that this backlash played a role in the reelection of Donald Trump.

What is the relevance to nature conservation? Trump won in ninety percent of American counties, including pretty much all the heavily rural ones, at least in the West. I will go out on a limb to suggest that when environmentalists—who tend to be among the educated and urban desk workers that al-Gharbi refers to as "symbolic capitalists"—demonize, antagonize, and speak as though we aspire to "cancel" farmers, ranchers, and hunters, the targets might take notice and vote accordingly, along with their rural friends and neighbors.

This wokeness dynamic can be heightened within progressive organizations. In his book *The Identity Trap*, political scientist Yascha Mounk writes that, "the pressure to conform becomes so strong that extremists gain the power to impose their views on everybody else." The performative contest of who is the most righteous (antiracist, vegan, misanthropic) has distracted organizations that have more important things to focus on. Similarly, land acknowledgements are these days a common performance before meetings and events of progressive organizations. But Jay Julius, former chairman of the Lummi Nation, is not a fan of them. He told me he "would rather hear a commitment to honor the treaties."

What does it mean to identify as an environmentalist or conservationist? Lifestyle choices such as recycling and minimizing our carbon footprint or meat consumption can shrink our individual impact on nature. That is good. But when such personal choices foster feelings of superiority toward others, identity is causing harm. I felt that toxic righteousness in my activist days, making me at times probably unsufferable to relatives. And I remember being indignant at slogans like *Every day is Earth Day for foresters (or farmers)*. There is indeed mischievous intent to such marketing, as though a forester or farmer can do no wrong. But the pragmatic response is to see it as more of an opportunity than as an offense to one's identity.

Remember my friend Mikal, or Doug Fir, from early in the book? After I left Earth First! for the journey I have described, he continued with edgy antics for a while. At one point, he dabbled in throwing pies at people. One target for a whipped cream delight was a statewide elected official who was addressing a forestry conference. Newspapers reported that the throw was a miss, glancing off the shoulder of his target. In years following, I collaborated with that man on forest issues and found him entirely reasonable and conservation-minded. One day early in Trump's first term, I ran into him in Seattle's Pike Place Market. We lamented the state of politics. Leaning close, he whispered, "Mitch, don't ever tell anybody that I used to be a Republican."

That calls to mind advice given by another old friend no longer with us, the renowned author and educator, Michael Frome. Michael liked to introduce me as a guest lecturer in his environmental journalism class at Western Washington University and often invited me to mix with student activists at potluck dinners in his home. He once said to me, "Don't burn bridges, because you don't know who your friends will be tomorrow." The years have affirmed his point, spotlighting the limitations of identity politics.

After four decades in conservation, including among the

most radical and enthusiastic true believers, I have only a hazy idea who the "good guys" are. With some exceptions, Team Green and Team Brown refuse to properly sort themselves.

I know liberals whose carbon footprint would shame a NASCAR driver. On the other hand, we know there are MAGA ranchers who work to coexist with wolves. Assumptions about other people and their values or interests foreclose options and opportunities. Hearts and minds do not change the future—actions do. I think we should work with everyone, not because we might change their opinions, but to learn what we can from them, to find common ground, and to do real work together to help the world.

A reason for the effectiveness of CNW is a culture that values pragmatism over virtue signaling. We are idealists (aspiring to accomplish important things like landscape conservation) but not idealogues. The CNW staff includes both urban vegans and rural hunters. Group discussions can be amusing and even uplifting. I observe mutual respect and affinity in how we relate to one another and to our community partners.

We can all make the active choice to get outside our own bubbles. I was lucky to have early jobs and life experiences that exposed me to ranchers, farmers, fishers, factory workers, and such. This may have given me an advantage in relating to diverse people. But I don't think it is too hard for urban progressives to seek out rural experiences or conservative relationships. The opposite is also true, as this is not only a matter of young progressives spending too much time with like-minded peers in latte cafes; it applies in spades to self-isolating rural conservatives. Farmers, ranchers, hunters, rural voices generally, along with their elected representatives, thrive on disparaging urban lifestyles and antagonizing urbanites and liberals. I don't know how long this has been so. Rural communities were once beneficiaries of New

Deal policies and voted blue accordingly, though I suspect they cast a side eye at the city even then. People are naturally suspicious of other lifestyles. But it makes no sense for conservationists to provoke and incite intensification of such views and accordant actions.

American views on wildlife and nature have been amply measured and documented. I have generalized about appreciation for nature being a common value among Americans, but it's more complicated than that. It would be naïve to believe that we all love grizzlies and wolves. Some scholars have studied values with respect to nature, placing them on a scale between "mutualist" and "traditionalist," with the latter being more utilitarian and viewing wildlife as subordinate. These views may be based on religion, culture, or the experience of living subject to harm from the vagaries of nature, like storms, floods, wildfire, and predation. Such values are durable and may hold sway among certain vocations, communities, and geographies indefinitely. But rare is the individual in which such values are absolute. I have found abundant common ground on love of nature with even very conservative and resource-dependent people.

Evolution bestowed us a mix of good and bad tendencies. Along with our identity baggage, we come pre-programmed with appreciation for nature (E.O. Wilson referred to this as *biophilia*) and invested in a healthy future. Also in the mix are feelings of greed and self-interest. We are all just fancy monkeys on a blue planet in a frozen universe, trying to make the best of our lives to the extent our evolutionary endowment will allow. As conservationists (with a small c, as a call to action rather than an identity), our job is to help draw out goodwill in partners and to find solutions that allow people to live more sustainably. Is one more likely to get there by forming relationships, finding where affinities (such as for wild nature) are shared, negotiating, and offering assistance, or by antagonizing and polarizing? To me the answer is obvious, both in the abstract and in my life experience.

I find great gratification and hope in my collaborative work at CNW. Still, there is no denying that conflict sells. It would be more fun and lucrative to be among the groups that perpetually campaign for false binary notions of perfection (e.g. no wolf or tree should die) and to rant at flawed government rather than to seek out diverse partnerships and solutions. The self-validation of identity lures people to want to *be* something more than to *do* something. The result is a culture war of choice even when solutions are at hand.

If you think of yourself as a hammer, everything looks like a nail. The incessant pounding has gotten old, and the rational basis for it is flawed. Set aside the identity politics and hubris, and what remains is the hard but rewarding work of finding solutions that sustain wildlife and nature while providing for prosperous and democratic human communities, both rural and urban. Pragmatic progress over identity. Doing something is better than being something.

Epilogue: Going Forward

I am a lucky dude. At age sixty-two, in the final third of my life, I am healthy and fulfilled. My kids are successful adults, my second marriage is happy and contenting, I am fit enough to play hoops every few days, and my material needs seem assured. While I remain an atheist with little religious inclination, I increasingly value my Jewish identity. I find comfort that my conservation contributions keep faith with the ancient Jewish calling of *tikkun olam*, to repair the world. I also live in my chosen home of western Washington, with its combination of economic prosperity and protected wild nature. If we can solve or at least forestall climate change, not to mention autocracy, I stand to have a sweet retirement. I can spend my golden years enjoying life on Puget Sound, between the stunning mountains of the Cascades and the Olympics, amid majestic forests and iconic wildlife that I helped conserve and restore.

In my fulfilling journey, I learned lessons that I hope will spread by my sharing here. I have learned that nature is not only or always fragile but can also be quite resilient if we give her a chance. Ways that we can better prepare to be effective toward solutions include exposing ourselves to a diversity of thought and experience, starting as early in life as possible. Resist the lure of identity. Seek out and genuinely listen to people with experience and views that differ from even your most cherished conceptions. Make those relationships real, not just transactional. And if you are trying to create political change, consider going about it indirectly. Instead of getting in the face of other stakeholders or the government with bullish demands, take the time to listen and search for common ground.

All this reminds me of a toy we used to get in Chicago's Chinatown when I was a kid. Called a Chinese finger trap, you jam fingers into either end of the tube, then try to pull them out. What you learn is that your fingers get freed not by pulling harder, but by pulling more gently. Looking back, I find that like with the Chinese finger trap, the more deliberate I became in my approach, the more nature I saved and at lower societal cost.

If you are an activist, aggressive tactics like blockading traffic or defacing art might feel cathartic but do not best serve your cause. If you lead a nonprofit organization whose website and press releases are a litany of lawsuits, ridicule, and demands of government, consider your other options. And if you are a supporter of nature conservation and find yourself donating to the red meat pitches that emphasize doom and disparage adversaries, I'm sorry, but you are doing it wrong. Instead of reinforcing the perverse incentives of polarization, seek out those spreading hope and finding solutions.

We need nature. Nobody can argue otherwise. The climate and biodiversity crises leave us little time to waste. Conservation must be a successful service that builds momentum and potential, not a performance to absolve egos. I believe there is hope and means for a future of civilized, democratic, prosperous society alongside and infused with wild nature. That is a mission we can strive toward together. For those who share this dream, I hope my story helps open pathways.

Over at CNW, we still have ideas to move forward.

Acknowledgements

I want to thank (but not blame) the following people for substantial editorial review of this book: Jon Gosch of Latah Books, James Johnston, Bettijean Collins, and Elizabeth Johnson. Tyler Ung and Andrea Wolf helped with graphics and photos. Also the following for review of the book in part or whole: Jackie Branz, Denis Hayes, David Weise, Don Stuart, Jasmine Minbashian, Ken Rait, Shelly Boyd, Daisy Purdy, Joe Scott, Paula Swedeen, Fred Munson, Jen Watkins, Sarah Lockenvitz, and Dana Lyons. I also want to express deep appreciation for the many unmentioned people who are part of this story, including staff, board members, donors, volunteers, and partners of Conservation Northwest.

About the Author

Mitch Friedman is a national leader in the conservation movement, known for his innovative and adaptive strategies. He serves as Executive Director of Seattle-based Conservation Northwest, which he founded in 1989. He has a degree in Zoology from the University of Washington and raised two daughters in Bellingham before moving back to Seattle, where he lives with his wife, Jackie, and their adopted dog, Wilma.

In his twenties, Mitch self-published two books about conservation. He also produced several campaign videos and a long-format video on the science of biodiversity that was used as a teaching aid in high school and college courses. Mitch was a founding board member of Wildlands Network and has served on several other conservation boards. He has been recognized with awards from Sunset Magazine, Society for Conservation Biology, The Wilderness Society, Washington Environmental Council, Northwest Jewish Environmental Project, Endangered Species Coalition, Wilburforce Foundation, and The Wildlife Society (NW Section). He has been profiled by the Seattle Times and, in 2003, he was named by *Washington Law and Politics Magazine* as one of the "25 smartest people in Washington." Mitch also volunteers with a group that raises funds to support the defense of Ukraine and is proud to be recognized as a NAFO "fella" for that work.

www.ingramcontent.com/pod-product-compliance
Lightning Source LLC
LaVergne TN
LVHW091205010425
807382LV00002B/10